Unseen, Overburdened, and Undervalued:
Navigating the Toxic Landscape of Family Caregiving

Julia Huckle

Published by Two Huckleberries Publishing

Copyright © Julia Huckle 2025
All rights reserved.

For Permission Requests, please contact:
Two Huckleberries Publishing
twohuckleberries@rogers.com

All rights reserved. No part of this publication may be reproduced, distributed, or transmitted in any form or by any means, including photocopying, recording, or other electronic or mechanical methods, without the prior written permission of the publisher, except in the case of brief quotations embodied in critical reviews and certain other noncommercial uses permitted by copyright law.

Julia Huckle
Ottawa, Ontario, Canada

ISBN:
Ebook: 978-1-0697912-0-7
Paperback: 978-1-0697912-3-8
Hard Cover Large Print: 978-1-0697912-2-1
Hard Cover Special Edition: 978-1-0697912-4-5

This book is dedicated to the one who made me a mum and a caregiver - my son Brandon. Heart, love, Bebe.

Table of Contents

Why I Wrote This Book and How To Use It	1
Prologue	4
Introduction	5
Chapter 1: Poor Communication	8
Chapter 2: Lack of Support	18
Chapter 3: Unhealthy Competition	31
Chapter 4: Lack of Recognition	41
Chapter 5: Micromanagement	50
Chapter 6: Favouritism and Discrimination	57
Chapter 7: Toxic Leadership	65
Chapter 8: High Levels of Stress and Burnout	74
Chapter 9: Lack of Work-Life Balance	83
Chapter 10: Excessive Workload, Unclear Expectations and Role Ambiguity	92
Chapter 11: Gossip and Negative Social Dynamics	105
Chapter 12: Inconsistent Workflows, Processes and Staffing	112
Chapter 13: Lack of Career Development Opportunities and Limited Training and Education	124
Chapter 14: Fear of Retaliation or Repercussions	131
Chapter 15: Lack of Transparency	139

Chapter 16: Unprofessional Behaviour and Harassment 145

Conclusion 153

Note from the Author 155

About the Author 156

Why I Wrote This Book and How To Use It

I have a professional me and my personal me. The book I originally intended to write was more personal. But I couldn't quite bring myself to open that door fully, and so I started with something that felt "safer." I've done a lot of reflection—because I'm still on my own healing journey while continuing to be both a caregiver and a professional.

Professionally, I've spent years working on burnout and the conditions that lead to it. My own experience with burnout happened in the personal realm, but like so many others, it eventually seeped into every part of my life—no matter how hard I tried to compartmentalize. What struck me most was how many of the contributing factors to professional burnout are the very same ones that contribute to caregiver burnout. And yet, in all the reading and research I've done, caregiver burnout is often treated differently. But why? It doesn't make sense to me.

I've come to believe that this disconnect is rooted in long-held biases, perceptions, and outdated beliefs—along with the history of how caregiving and healthcare have evolved. There's this false divide that places caregivers outside the professional realm. But I've sat at similar tables as both a caregiver and a professional. I'm the same person. I bring the same knowledge, skills, education, and experiences. The only difference—aside from the hat I happen to be wearing—is how others at the table perceive me.

So what if we viewed caregiver burnout through the same lens we use for professional burnout? What if I applied the well-documented, research-based contributing factors to my own experiences—and to what I've witnessed and heard from others? What might that reveal? What could it change?

This book is not about blaming or shaming anyone.

As a professional, I know what we're taught, what we experience, and how much we contend with inside our systems and structures. That, too, became a source of burnout for me. Because I also knew —deeply—that the people who needed help the most often didn't get it in time. I know the ache of not being able to do enough for the people in our care. And I know the sting of being on the receiving end of words and actions—those moments where I sent an apology out into the universe, hoping I hadn't once said or done the thing that had just wounded me. Not because I was a bad person. But because of what I had learned. Because of what I hadn't yet learned. Because of what I still don't have words for.

The stories shared here are not about blaming or criticizing individual professionals or organizations. That doesn't solve anything. In fact, I believe it only makes things worse. Most of us want the same thing: to be the best we can be and to offer the best care possible to those we serve. In fact, the recommendations are also inspired by caregivers and professionals further emphasizing the desire and willingness for change.

While writing this book, I asked others to read, reflect, review, and offer feedback. I am deeply grateful for their insight and care. This book is stronger because of them. Two questions in particular stayed with me:

1. Are the stories real?
2. Why aren't the quotes attributed?

The stories are real. The quotes are real. Just like the ongoing struggles of caregiving are real. So, too, are the fears—of retaliation, of blame and shame, of not being believed. I hold a strong commitment to both writing integrity and confidentiality. To protect the emotional safety and trust of those who shared their experiences, I chose to leave quotes and stories unattributed and anonymized. That decision has been respected and appreciated by those involved. I also chose to use the words "person" or "person requiring care" and similar language to acknowledge and respect the complexity and nature of the variety of relationships between caregivers and their person. It is not always family and the other dynamics are complicated.

This book is meant to invite reflection, discussion, and conversation. Each chapter is written to stand alone so when you find yourself in a situation, you know where to turn.

The curriculum developer, professor, and guest speaker in me hopes students will use this book to spark learning while they're still forming their professional identity. I hope professionals will use it to reflect on their own experiences—and to consider how they might help improve things for caregivers. Because when we support caregivers, we improve patient care and safety. We also improve our own satisfaction at work which in turn prevents burnout. I hope workplaces will find ways to better support caregivers—whether they're employees or connected to someone receiving care. I hope policy-makers and funders will see the irreplaceable contribution of family caregivers and invest in protecting them. I hope advocates and allies will find language and courage to amplify caregiver voices. And I hope caregivers feel a little less alone, and find something here that helps them carry the weight just a bit more easily.

As you move through the book—or reflect on it later—I'd love to hear what stands out for you. I've set up a dedicated email address where you can share your thoughts: *unseen_comments@rogers.com.*

Prologue

"In Canada, 1 in 4 people care for an aging or disabled loved one and half of Canadians will be a caregiver at some point in their lives. But what isn't reported is the staggering number of caregivers who suffer in silence, overwhelmed by stress, mental health struggles, and toxic dynamics, without any real support. And yet, few are ever offered a roadmap to navigate the toxic, often soul-crushing dynamics that arise. We've all heard the terms 'toxic work culture' and 'workplace burnout,' but when it comes to caregiving, there are no guidelines, no systemic supports, and no easy answers."

"In many cultures, caregivers are seen as selfless heroes, but in reality, they are often the invisible victims of a system that fails to recognize their needs. While companies are now investing in anti-toxic workplace policies and mental health support, caregivers are often punished for asking for the very support that is supposed to exist. In the real world, caregiving is a trap that many cannot escape, and the very systems that should be rescuing them are the ones ensnaring them further."

I hope this book will ignite the change that is needed.

Introduction

Toxic workplaces are a familiar subject: environments where employees feel overworked, unsupported, and isolated. They battle burnout, toxic leadership, a lack of support, emotional strain, high staff turnover, inadequate work/life balance, and a lack of resources, often with little recourse. Employees want to be seen, heard and valued and when the environment doesn't support this, it creates challenges for employees and employers. Organizations focus on strategies to improve these cultures: leadership training, wellness initiatives, and Employee Assistance Programs. Employees are encouraged to 'speak up,' 'set boundaries,' and practice 'resilience.' When they face burnout or toxic behaviour, they are told they can seek help or even leave if the environment becomes too damaging.

But what happens when you can't leave? For caregivers, those who provide care out of love or duty rather than as paid care providers or professionals, the challenges extend far beyond the typical workplace. They juggle caregiving duties in their homes while also dealing with systems and institutions that are meant to support their loved one and to a lesser extent the caregiver, yet can also worsen their struggles. Caregivers are expected to advocate for their loved ones, but this advocacy can come at a steep price: risking retaliation, losing essential services for their loved one, or even jeopardizing their own role as caregivers. This creates a paradox: caregivers must navigate toxic behaviours and structures in complex systems, but speaking up within those systems may leave them with fewer resources and more isolation.

Family caregivers face not only the strain of caregiving, but a web of fragmented services that are often underfunded and overwhelmed. Unlike paid employees, caregivers don't have the luxury of walking away from their roles, even at the end of the day. They live their responsibilities day in and day out, without the same protections or recognition that employees might expect in the workplace.

As we consider caregiver burnout, we must look at it through the same lens as workplace burnout, but with one crucial distinction: caregiving isn't a job you can clock out of. Caregivers fill many roles, beyond completing care tasks, such as managers, coordinators, and advocates, yet their labour is often invisible to the systems they rely on. What if we evaluated the caregiver's experience the same way we evaluate workplace culture? Caregivers are not just "helping out," they are performing high-stress, essential work under toxic conditions, often without the resources or support they need. Too frequently, they are labeled as "difficult" or "hard to serve" when they struggle, deepening their isolation and eroding their confidence.

Resilience is often proposed as the solution to these challenges. But while resilience is valuable, it's not a cure for systemic failure. Caregivers cannot be expected to endure harm simply because the system is broken. Shifting the burden of resilience onto caregivers deepens their distress and misplaces the responsibility for change.

The struggles faced by caregivers are not isolated to Canada; they are felt worldwide. And the COVID-19 pandemic only amplified these challenges, pushing caregivers further to the margins, their needs ignored, and their efforts dismissed. Trust in systems eroded, and many caregivers lost access to the resources that once helped them.

But this isn't a story of defeat, it's one of perseverance, with hope and determination. Despite the toxicity they face, caregivers continue to fight for dignity and the recognition they deserve. This book is not just for caregivers; it's a call to action for professionals, organizations, and policymakers to step in and make real, lasting change.

The systems meant to support caregivers must change. It's time for all of us - caregivers, professionals, organizations, and policymakers - to come together and create systems that are supportive, sustainable, and fair. The policies we create today will shape the caregiving experience tomorrow. We must do better.

Chapter 1: Poor Communication

"There is so much to keep track of when you are a caregiver. And then you have to be the one to keep track of it all and run around and share it with everyone. Why can't providers talk to each other? I've signed so many consent forms and still it falls to me. And then there are times when they do talk to each other but the information is very different than what I was told. Which is the correct information? Where are the mistakes happening? Is it me?"

When communication is unclear, inconsistent, or absent, it leads to confusion, frustration, and misunderstandings. At its most fundamental level, it destroys trust. Family caregivers, who often rely on information from a variety of sources (healthcare professionals, organizations, family members, and the individuals they care for), experience these communication breakdowns regularly. This lack of clear communication can result in mistakes, delays in care, and an overwhelming sense of being underprepared or unsupported. Therefore, it affects safety of the person receiving care. Misunderstandings between caregivers and medical professionals can complicate an already stressful caregiving role, making the experience even more difficult.

This chapter addresses how poor communication affects caregivers and explores practical solutions for caregivers, healthcare professionals, organizations, and policymakers to improve communication and reduce stress.

Examples:

Management of a service agency that provides frequent and varied supports for Fred, a disabled adult, fails to update their team on company changes, leading to rumours or incorrect assumptions amongst staff. Fred's parents hear rumours but receive no formal communication about changes and how it will impact them, Fred, and the services they receive. This creates a lot of stress and uncertainty leading to poor sleep and disrupted focus on other tasks and responsibilities.

Tom attends a doctor's appointment with his wife for whom he provides care, and they receive verbal instructions but no written documentation. Later, Tom is told they misunderstood the care instructions of what to watch for, which resulted in a medication error. The lack of follow-up leaves Tom in a vulnerable position, unsure of how to manage the situation.

Edna has dementia and lives in a long term care home. Her needs change frequently, but the caregiver isn't kept up to date on the changes. This results in confusion about Edna's behaviour and needs and her caregiver is uncertain about her ability to make informed decisions.

A case worker fails to explain the eligibility criteria for services clearly, leaving the caregiver to navigate the complicated application process. The caregiver completes and submits the extensive paperwork on their own, only to find out that they weren't eligible at all.

A receptionist from an organization to which a referral for supports was sent 18 months ago, calls a caregiver to make an appointment and to provide and confirm information. They mumble and speak quickly rattling off the standard message, and the caregiver, who was busy when the call came through, asks the receptionist to repeat where they were from and what this was regarding. The receptionist's voice shows clear annoyance about having to repeat the information and asks the caregiver "don't you remember that this referral was sent?"

The government implements a new benefit for people with disabilities. Sally is sent a letter regarding her daughter's eligibility for the benefit and the online registration process. Sally goes online, follows the instructions, and after completing several screens and clicking submit, is taken to a screen directing them to call the office in order to be able to complete the registration. Sally feels discouraged and overwhelmed. Unable to find time during office hours to make a call of indeterminant length, the task sits undone for months. This means she spends money on services that she can't afford and should be covered by the program.

A social worker has met with a struggling family that is in desperate need of support. She knows that the family doesn't meet the criteria for many services and the few that they do have very long waitlists. She feels horrible that she can't help and avoids reaching out to the family to give them this news. This leaves the family waiting in the abyss of the unknown and feeling abandoned. Further, it wastes time that they could use filling out the application forms to get on the waitlists and talking to others that may be able to offer alternative ideas and supports.

Recommendations for Family Caregivers:

- **Clarify Information**: Always ask for written instructions when receiving medical advice or care plans to avoid

misunderstandings and to have a clear reference point for later.
- **Document**: Keep a caregiving journal or log of important dates, changes in care, and medications. This will help maintain a sense of control, reduce confusion, and help reduce the mental load of caregiving.
- **Ask for Copies of Reports**: Request and maintain copies of reports. Read through them for accuracy of information and address any errors or omissions. You can also request to review charts and files if you have concerns.
- **Advocate**: Don't hesitate to follow up with healthcare providers to ensure they have communicated everything clearly and that you fully understand the care plan.
- **Be Proactive**: If you haven't received an important update or instruction, take the initiative to ask questions and request follow-up communication.
- **Create a Communication Plan**: Establish a clear communication plan with family members, organizations and care providers to ensure everyone is updated and on the same page.
- **Record Conversations**: When discussing medical care, it may help to record the conversation (with permission) to refer back to later for clarity.
- **Write It Down**: Come to appointments prepared with your questions and information you want to share written down. This will help not only keep you organized but will also make sure you don't forget things when you have so much going on all at once. Having a paper handy will also let you jot down any important information in the same place.
- **Ask for Help**: Seek out organizations and employees that offer information sessions about new initiatives and the processes involved. For complex issues, legal or accounting advice may be beneficial.

Recommendations for Professionals:

- **Provide Clear Instructions**: Always provide written documentation of verbal instructions, and check that caregivers understand them. Use the Teachback method to support caregiver understanding. The Teachback method is one where the teacher has the learner teach them the information so that they can determine if the information was properly explained and understood and if any clarifications or corrections are needed. This also helps the learner feel more comfortable and confident in the information that they have learned.
- **Check-in Regularly**: Offer regular check-ins and set up follow-up appointments with caregivers to answer questions and provide updates on care plans.
- **Collaborate with Caregivers**: Engage caregivers in care discussions as partners in the care planning process, making sure they feel valued and heard.
- **Use Plain Language**: Avoid medical jargon, acronyms or complicated language and explain things in simple, accessible terms to ensure caregivers fully understand instructions. Provide contact information to caregivers when making referrals for supports and services. This will allow the caregiver to follow-up with them to ask questions or get further information.
- **Implement Follow-Up Mechanisms**: Implement structured follow-up mechanisms such as calls or electronic messaging to caregivers after significant care decisions are made in order to verify understanding, address concerns, and answer any follow-up questions. Check with the caregiver to see which method is preferred.
- **Teach Communication and Advocacy Skills**: Offer workshops to caregivers on how to communicate

effectively with healthcare teams and ask the right questions.
- **Engage in Active Listening**: Professionals should practice active listening techniques, validating caregivers' concerns and ensuring their voices are heard.
- **Prepare for Appointments with Follow-Up Questions Based on the Previous Visit**: This shows that you actively listened to the caregiver and allows you to follow-up on progress, changes, implementation of any actions, follow-up on referrals and other elements of the care plan. It can also help you anticipate questions that the caregiver may have.
- **Timely Communication**: Information that is common for professionals can be overwhelming for caregivers, especially when they not only need time to absorb and make sure they understand it, but also to formulate and ask questions, then process those answers. There can be many other implications for the caregiver, and the person they care for, that need to be carefully considered before fully informed decisions can be made.
- **Focus on Care Versus Cure:** Recognize that you don't need to have all of the answers and solutions in order to be able to help someone. Open and honest conversations about what is available and active listening provide benefits to caregivers. Taking a coaching approach to find out what the caregiver thinks would help and be understanding that when they don't know, it can be for a variety of reasons: nobody has asked them and they haven't thought about it; people have let them down; they don't know what is available out there to help them; they may need assistance to think creatively; and, more. Thinking creatively can be a tremendous support. While you may not be able to shorten waitlists or create services that don't exist or fix staffing shortages, sometimes by thinking of supports and services

that will take other pressures off the caregiver can be even more beneficial. For example, housekeeping can free up the caregiver's time to run an errand or complete paperwork. Batch cooking can relieve shopping time and the chore of cooking on hard days. However, one of the barriers of this can be a lack of freezer and fridge space. Can the caregiver be supported to purchase a used freezer at a low cost and then assisted with delivery of it? This task would seem overwhelming to an already stressed caregiver but the long term benefits are immense. Communication is essential for working with caregivers to find realistic and actionable solutions.

Recommendations for Organizations:

- **Provide Communication Training**: Provide training for staff on clear communication strategies ensuring a consistent approach across departments, particularly for caregivers to be informed and supported. Include any policies relating to caregiver communication in orientations of all new staff.
- **Utilize Technology**: Implement secure patient portals where caregivers can easily access medical records, prescriptions, instructions, and updates in a caregiver-friendly format. Provide paper copies as well without assuming internet access and technological savviness. Technology can also be used for secure messaging to send caregivers instructions or information obtained after the appointment and allow caregivers to upload data e.g. blood pressure readings, at a convenient time for them in preparation for appointments.
- **Utilize Consistency**: Assign a single point of contact (e.g. case manager) to caregivers to improve continuity in communication. Ensuring that a primary caregiver is

identified and all information is shared with them, will assist with consistency in two-way information sharing.
- **Create Care Coordination Teams**: Develop care coordination teams that are specifically dedicated to facilitating communication between healthcare providers, patients, and caregivers. Coordinated care plans that are shared between multiple providers, patients and caregivers will align goals of care and action items reducing duplication and gaps. For complex clients, circle of care meetings might be beneficial to develop and follow-up on coordinated care plans.
- **Provide Regular Updates**: Ensure caregivers receive regular updates on their loved one's progress, treatment, and any changes to the care plan. Scheduling these in advance and at a regular cadence at a time that works for the caregiver can help with organization and planning and prevent gaps in communication.
- **Provide Communication Support for Patient/Caregiver Information**: For information that can be generalized, pre-written booklets or information sheets with room for customization can benefit from a review by a communications and health education team. This will provide a safety measure for language level, use of common language, accuracy of information, templating, translation, and more. This allows for more time reviewing and customizing information while answering questions instead of spending it writing things out.
- **Develop Policies Regarding Caregiver Communication**: Embed caregiver communication actions in policies and procedures. Write specific policies and procedures to ensure a robust plan and to set expectations for staff.
- **Link to Patient/Client Safety**: Communication with caregivers should be a key component to patient safety plans and initiatives.

- **Develop Accreditation Standards**: Accreditation organizations should include standards regarding communication with caregivers.

Recommendations for Policy Makers:

- **Ensure Accessibility of Information**: Ensure that communication is compliant with accessibility standards, taking into consideration potential language barriers, disabilities, or technological limitations.
- **Introduce Mandated Requirements**: Introduce ministry mandates and regulations that require health and social service systems to provide caregivers with accessible, detailed written and verbal care instructions.
- **Invest in Data Sharing and Interoperability Policies**: Create policies and fund implementation projects that facilitate secure and seamless sharing of information between healthcare providers, patients, and caregivers, with caregiver consent.
- **Increase Public Awareness**: Launch campaigns that highlight the importance of clear communication in caregiving, to improve understanding across healthcare systems and society at large.
- **Develop and Implement Communication Plans**: Ensure that all government and program websites are user friendly and provide clear information for caregivers. Offer information sessions, support lines and other tools for those that need additional support.

Key Takeaways:

1. **Communication is Vital**: Clear, consistent communication is crucial for effective caregiving and prevents mistakes, enhancing patient safety.

2. **Proactive Communication**: Caregivers should take a proactive approach by asking questions and following up with providers when communication is unclear.
3. **Documentation is Key**: Keeping a log of medical advice, changes in care, and important information will help caregivers stay organized and avoid confusion.
4. **Professional Support**: Professionals must prioritize clear communication with caregivers, ensuring they feel heard and included in decision-making.
5. **Organizational Responsibility**: Organizations should create systems that foster effective communication with caregivers, from training staff to using technology to enhancing information flow.
6. **Patient Safety**: Communication affects patient/client safety. As key partners in care, caregivers must be considered in the development and implementation of patient safety plans and initiatives.

Summary:

Poor communication can severely hinder a caregiver's ability to provide the best care and can lead to burnout, confusion, and mistakes. By taking steps to clarify, document, and advocate for clear communication, caregivers can feel more confident and supported. Professionals and organizations can play a vital role in improving communication, which in turn helps alleviate the stress caregivers face. Clear, consistent communication should be seen as a fundamental part of effective caregiving, ensuring both the caregiver and the person they care for receive the best possible and safest care.

Chapter 2: Lack of Support

"Behind closed doors, millions of caregivers are silently suffocating under the weight of toxic relationships and systems that were never designed to support them. But what if the real 'illness' is not the person they care for — but the system that ignores their needs?"

Caregivers often find themselves navigating their responsibilities without sufficient emotional, practical, or logistical support. The absence of consistent support systems leaves caregivers feeling overwhelmed, isolated, and burned out. Many caregivers are expected to perform complex tasks without adequate resources, guidance, or assistance. While paid care providers and professionals can access mental health days, time off, or employee assistance programs, caregivers are largely left without similar protections or support structures. This chapter delves into the emotional and practical toll that a lack of support has on caregivers and highlights the ways both individuals and systems can work to improve this aspect of caregiving.

Examples:

Sarah, a family caregiver to her elderly mother, finds herself constantly juggling caregiving duties with a full-time job and household responsibilities. When she asks family members for help, they offer excuses, express indifference, or offer little more than superficial words of encouragement. They say, "You're doing a great job," but no one offers to help with the practical aspects, such as cooking meals or helping with cleaning. Sarah feels like she is constantly struggling without any respite. Day program and business hours of organizations and providers already cut into her work hours which quickly uses up any vacation or sick time. This means Sarah has to make difficult choices between further work and financial implications and getting supports and services.

Maria has been a sole caregiver for her daughter with special needs for several years. She is emotionally and physically drained, but she hesitates to ask for help, fearing that others won't understand the depth of her struggle. She battles feelings of guilt, thinking that asking for assistance would make her seem incapable. When she reaches a breaking point and asks for respite care from a local support service, she's told there's a long waiting list or that they're not eligible due to restrictive guidelines. Other available options are either too expensive or don't meet her specific needs, leaving her nowhere to turn.

Mark works full-time as a teacher while also caring for his disabled brother. The few hours of caregiving respite he can access are during his work hours, meaning he is forced to choose between attending to his caregiving duties or his career. He has little flexibility to care for his own health and well-being without facing serious work-related consequences. He applies for financial assistance programs to help with out-of-pocket medical costs, but the application process is so complex and time-consuming that he gives up before getting any help. When he asks his brother's case manager for help with the application he is told "you have to help yourself."

Kelly reaches out to their own health care provider for mental health support related to caregiving overwhelm and fatigue. The provider gives the caregiver a pep talk and recommends that the caregiver "do yoga". No referral or list of resources is provided for her to get out to "do yoga" making it an impractical solution. Assessments for stress, anxiety and depression are not completed and no medications are discussed. She is left to manage her emotional strain on her own. The healthcare system doesn't provide a clear path for caregivers to access mental health support or counselling services, leaving caregivers to manage their emotional stress without professional help.

Rebecca maintains a full time job on top of caregiving duties for her aging mother and maintaining a household. Everything falls to her unless she can find the funds to pay for services such as lawn care, snow shovelling, and more. Slowly things fall behind leading to criticism of her ability to maintain inside and outside the home. The thought of clearing things out is overwhelming, even if she could even find the time and energy. Someone complains to the City about the lawn. Someone else calls them hoarders. When a neighbour does come over to mow the lawn once, the tears of gratitude are also mixed with despair.

Recommendations for Family Caregivers:

- **Seek Help**: Don't be afraid to ask for support, whether from family, friends, or local caregiving organizations. You are not expected to do it all on your own.
- **Get Respite**: Take breaks, even if it's just for a few hours, to avoid burnout.
- **Join Support Groups**: Connect with other caregivers for emotional support and practical advice. Reach out to support groups, either in person or online, where you can connect with other caregivers who understand the emotional strain of caregiving.
- **Create a Support Network**: Build a support system of family, friends, and other caregivers who can offer advice, emotional support, or even hands-on help when needed.

- **Utilize Technology**: Use caregiving apps to track appointments, medications, and tasks, which can reduce your stress, help you stay organized and decrease the mental load.
- **Access Community Resources**: Look for and explore local caregiving resources and community-based services like meal delivery programs, transportation services, adult daycare options that can provide a break, respite care, support groups, and nonprofit organizations that can offer help. Community resources may also include housekeeping, lawn care, snow shovelling, meal or grocery delivery to preserve your energy for other tasks and allow time for restorative care.
- **Ask for Time Off**: If you are balancing caregiving with a job, talk to your employer about adjusting your hours or responsibilities to allow more time for caregiving. Explore various types of available leave that are offered by your employer. Work from home options may increase the amount of time for yourself due to the reduction in commuting time.
- **Talk to a Therapist**: Consider professional counselling or therapy to help manage stress, anxiety, and other emotions. Many caregivers overlook their own mental health needs.
- **Make Time for Yourself**: Prioritize restorative care and take breaks. Even short moments of restorative care, such as enjoying a cup of tea, taking a walk, doing a hobby, or as seemingly little as a minute of deep breathing, can make a significant difference in your emotional well-being.
- **Acknowledge Your Feelings**: Accept that it's normal to feel frustrated, sad, or overwhelmed. Finding healthy outlets, like journaling or speaking with a trusted friend, can help you process these feelings.

- **Ask for Referrals**: If you're unsure where to seek help, don't hesitate to ask healthcare professionals for local resources or support services.
- **Leverage Online Tools**: Use online tools, apps, and websites that offer caregiver advice, resources, and community support.
- **Take Time To Understand Your Needs**: It is easy to lose track of yourself and what you need when you are consumed with caring for someone else and prioritizing their needs over your own. We also get used to people telling us what support is available versus what we need. Take some time to think about what would help YOU. Then look at who might be able to help make it possible. It's ok to refuse "help" that doesn't really help you.
- **Learn to Accept Help**: While it can be difficult, learning to trust others and accept their help is a vital step in your caregiving journey. Maintaining boundaries around what you need and will find helpful and when it works for you can assist with finding the right supporter.
- **Lead with Trust**: This is a hard one. I absolutely would never recommend that caregivers blindly trust, especially when we have had our trust tested and broken so many times. I am suggesting that for our own health and well-being, we need to trust that there are good people, professionals, and organizations out there that can and will help us. We need to have enough trust in them to let go of our fears and trauma. We need to be able to heal and keep caring for our loved ones. As a nurse I looked caregivers in the eyes when they were dropping off their loved one to respite and asked them to trust me. Only after becoming a caregiver, can I fully understood the strength that it takes to give someone that trust.

"In a typical workplace, employees can file complaints, request mental health days, or even change teams. They can leave the job if the environment becomes unbearable. But for caregivers, who is there to listen? Where are the policies that protect them from burnout? What programs offer them time off, therapy, or support groups? The truth is, there is no Employee Assistance Program for family caregivers."

Recommendations for Professionals:

- **Provide Resources and Referrals for Practical Support**: Direct caregivers to local resources, including respite care, support groups and peer support networks, counselling services, or caregiver workshops that can help provide support. If you offer caregivers a comprehensive list of available community resources, such as home health services, financial assistance programs, or support groups, highlight the ones that they will be eligible for and provide information such as potential wait times and application processes, and help them navigate complex systems to receive the assistance they need. When possible, refer caregivers to specialized services, like mental health counselling or financial advising, that can help alleviate some of their stress. Remember that supports are most beneficial when they are what the caregivers, wants and needs and happens when they need it.
- **Listen**: Acknowledge the emotional and physical strain caregivers are under, and work with the caregiver to find practical solutions that might help.
- **Develop and Maintain a Trusting Relationship**: Build rapport and maintain open lines of communication with

caregivers. This fosters trust and creates an environment where caregivers feel comfortable asking for help.
- **Offer Validation**: Ensure caregivers feel appreciated and recognized for their role, which helps reduce isolation.
- **Normalize and Encourage Restorative Care**: Discuss the importance of self-care regularly with caregivers and encourage them to take time for themselves to avoid burnout. Provide information on coping strategies and stress management techniques that are practical for that caregiver and their situation.
- **Offer Emotional Support**: Recognize and validate caregivers' emotional challenges. Offering reassurance and encouragement can help caregivers feel supported.
- **Provide Check-ins**: During medical visits or care consultations, make it a point to check in on the emotional and psychological well-being of the caregiver. Offer resources for mental health support when needed.
- **Discuss Practical Restorative Care Options**: Encourage caregivers to recognize the importance of taking care of their own mental health.
- **Create Safe Spaces for Discussion**: Foster an environment where caregivers feel comfortable discussing their emotional challenges, knowing that their feelings are validated and supported.

Recommendations for Organizations:

- **Encourage Respite Options**: Offer, develop partnerships, or connect caregivers to respite care options that allow them to take necessary breaks to recharge and focus on their own health without worrying about their loved one's care.
- **Place an Emphasis on Family-Centred Care**: Create a caregiving environment that involves family members in

care planning and decision-making so they feel like supported and valued members of the team.
- **Provide Training**: Provide training programs for caregivers, teaching them effective caregiving skills, stress management, and self-care. Make it accessible and practical for already strained caregivers.
- **Offer Flexible Work Policies**: Offer flexible work hours or telecommuting options to employees who are also caregivers, reducing the stress of managing both roles. Explore other policies and initiatives that support Caregivers-Friendly Workplace practices and Burnout Prevention Programs.
- **Develop Caregiver Assistance Programs**: Set up programs specifically designed to help caregivers, such as counselling, financial planning assistance, and legal advice. Seek out employee benefit packages that include services and other benefits for caregivers.
- **Offer Caregiver Support Groups**: Organize or partner with local mental health professionals to host caregiver support groups where emotional support is available in a structured environment.
- **Offer Paid Time Off Options for Caregivers**: Provide employees who are caregivers with paid time off to attend to their loved ones' medical needs or to take care of their own health. Explore options in benefits packages.
- **Provide Training to Staff:** Provide training to staff on how to treat caregivers as partners in care, walk alongside them, and share existing resources available to caregivers. Allow staff extra time to incorporate this training into the patient appointments.
- **Provide Training to Staff (Human Resources and peers):** Caregivers should feel safe disclosing their caregiving responsibilities to Human Resources, leaders, and their peers. Training for all members of organizations

on how to talk with their co-workers about caregiving, offer support, and increase everyone's knowledge and skills around caregiving topics and realities will help create a culture of caring and a caregiver-friendly workplace.
- **Promote Mental Health Resources**: Make mental health resources, including counselling services and stress-relief workshops, readily available to caregivers.
- **Implement Peer Mentoring Programs**: Pair new caregivers with experienced ones for emotional support, offering guidance and empathy through shared experiences.
- **Provide In-House Support**: Offer on-site services like counselling or financial planning for caregivers, or develop partnerships with local organizations to provide these services.
- **Streamline Resource Access**: Create a one-stop resource hub that caregivers can access to find all the support they need, from physical care options to emotional support programs.
- **Collaborate with Nonprofits**: Partner with nonprofit organizations that offer services like financial aid, respite care, and caregiver training to provide a more robust support network.
- **Become an Employer of Choice for Caregivers**: Caregiver burnout will impact a caregiver's work life. Burnout in one area can expedite the onset, increase the breadth and depth of symptoms, and prolong the length of burnout in other areas, including the workplace. Burnout prevention strategies should include those that support caregiver needs beyond the workplace. Utilize mechanisms such as Employee Resource Groups and Workplace Safety to help fund and sustain programs and initiatives.
- **Start and Maintain Employee Resource Groups (ERGs)**: Consider whether your organization would benefit from an ERG and how — whether communicating

supports; offering resources such as connecting lunches, financial planning and other information sessions, and caregiver coaches; and, reviewing company changes from the lens of a caregiver.

Recommendations for Policy Makers:

- **Support Legislation that Assists Caregivers**: Advocate for paid family leave, respite care funding, and other policies that relieve the burden on caregivers.
- **Fund Community Programs**: Fund community-based programs to ensure that caregivers have access to support services close to home.
- **Increase Funding for Caregiver Support**: Allocate government funds to support respite care programs, caregiver education, and financial assistance for caregivers.
- **Enhance Self-Directed Funding Programs:** Self-directed funding is limited and there are very strict parameters. And yet, this is one way to provide flexibility to caregivers and to help them overcome barriers to accessing already limited supports and services. By opening up the parameters around this funding, caregivers and their supporting professionals can think more creatively and find alternate ways of getting help.
- **Expand Paid Family Leave**: Ensure that paid family leave is available to caregivers, regardless of their employment status, to help balance caregiving and work responsibilities.
- **Introduce New and Enhance Current Tax Relief Programs**: Introduce tax credits and deductions for family caregivers to help alleviate the financial strain of caregiving responsibilities. Review current programs for barriers and potential for enhancements to make them more accessible while reducing red tape. This can include enhancing medical and support expenses programs that already exist.

- **Fund Caregiver Education Programs**: Implement caregiver education programs that offer training and resources, enhancing the skills and confidence of family caregivers.
- **Fund Caregiver Mental Health Services**: Invest in programs that offer free or low-cost mental health support specifically for family caregivers. Provide access to therapy, counselling, or stress management workshops. Caregiver coaches can provide numerous benefits to caregivers and help them feel more confident and supported in their caregiving role.
- **Integrate Emotional Support for Caregivers into Care Plans**: Advocate for policies that incorporate emotional support services as part of formal care plans for caregivers supporting those individuals with long-term or complex care needs.
- **Launch and Sustain Public Awareness Campaigns**: Raise awareness about the emotional burden of caregiving through public campaigns, highlighting the importance of seeking mental health support. Develop campaigns to raise awareness about available caregiver resources and how to access them.
- **Provide Paid Leave for Mental Health**: Implement policies that allow caregivers to take paid leave for mental health reasons, helping them recover from burnout and maintain their emotional well-being.
- **Expand Eligibility for Assistance**: Work to broaden the eligibility for caregiver assistance programs, ensuring that more families can access critical support.
- **System Funding**: Strained and underfunded systems such as health and social services offload tasks and responsibilities onto caregivers, often without supporting caregivers to take on these tasks. We need to address

system challenges and support professionals so they in turn can support caregivers.
- **Leverage Existing Programs:** Occupational Health and Safety (OH&S) legislation already includes language around psychological safety. This could be leveraged to include disclosing caregiver responsibilities and working together to accommodate caregiving while meeting operational needs. If caregivers do not feel safe disclosing their caregiving responsibilities for fear of discrimination for projects, promotions, attendance at conferences, networking, and other opportunities, then there should be mechanisms to support them. Further, OH&S can cover disclosure of things such as not being able to work when incapacitated by a lack of sleep due to caregiving responsibilities.

Key Takeaways:

1. **Caregivers Need Support:** The lack of emotional and practical support is one of the primary contributors to caregiver burnout. Caregivers need access to a wide array of resources to help them manage the emotional and physical toll of caregiving.
2. **Restorative Care is Essential:** Caregivers need to prioritize their well-being, whether through taking breaks, seeking help, or connecting with mental health professionals.
3. **Community and Family Support Matter:** Building a support network of family, friends, and fellow caregivers is crucial in alleviating stress and preventing burnout.
4. **Organizations and Professionals Can Help:** Healthcare providers, employers, and organizations must recognize the importance of supporting caregivers and offering resources to make their lives more manageable.

5. **Policy Change is Needed:** Policymakers must enact laws that provide caregivers with paid leave, mental health support, and financial relief to ensure they are not left to shoulder caregiving responsibilities alone.

Summary:

Caregivers are often expected to bear the weight of responsibility without adequate support, which leads to overwhelming stress, burnout, and isolation. It is crucial that both systems and individuals recognize the need for practical and emotional support to ensure caregivers can continue their important roles while also maintaining their well-being. Through a combination of self-care, professional assistance, community support, and systemic change, caregivers can receive the recognition and resources they need to thrive.

Chapter 3: Unhealthy Competition

"I completed the multipage application for service and waited. And waited. I knew there were long wait lists. I figured that was the reason why I never heard back. I was desperate for help but thought that there must be a lot of people worse off if I wasn't getting a call. I was so desperate that I called to find out what was happening. I was told that we didn't qualify for service based on the form I completed. I had waited over a year! Why did nobody tell me? All that time spent on the paperwork and then waiting....for nothing."

Unhealthy competition in caregiving environments doesn't simply emerge from within families. It may be actively fostered by the professionals and systems meant to support caregivers. When caregivers are excluded from decision-making or dismissed as "less knowledgeable" than the "expert" or "professional" care team, it creates an environment where they feel undermined, marginalized, under valued, and, in some cases, locked in competition for resources, attention, acknowledgement, and respect. Rather than collaborating, professionals and caregivers find themselves in opposition, with caregivers feeling they must "prove" their value. This competition makes caregiving even more exhausting and demoralizing, leading to frustration, burnout, and a lack of trust in the health and social services systems.

Competition can also occur over scarce health and social services resources. "If mental health is the poor cousin of healthcare than addictions is the poor cousin of mental health." Families compete against each other for resources. Professionals must advocate on behalf of some of their clients at the risk of others. Organizations are also competing against other organizations. It is at every level. The centre of it is the patient/client and caught up in the storm is the caregiver. Because they are the "poor cousin" of the patient/client.

This chapter examines how unhealthy competition is cultivated not only by family dynamics but also by the professionals and institutional systems that are supposed to assist. It provides examples of how this competition can manifest and offers recommendations for how caregivers, professionals, organizations, and policymakers can work together to create a more collaborative and supportive caregiving environment.

Examples:

Frank and Ted are both caregivers for their parents, Mary and Alfred, and attend appointments together as much as they can so that they both get the same and accurate information. Frequently, the doctor and social worker give priority to Frank's opinions and ideas, because he is the one who is more assertive, dismissing the input or concerns of Ted, Mary and Alfred. This leads to friction in the family and Mary and Alfred going along with what Frank suggests.

Sarah has been a primary caregiver for her father for years and has maintained power of attorney for her father even though he is now in long-term care. She has been deeply involved in his care and has a clear understanding of his preferences. However, when she tries to contribute her knowledge to the care plan, the care team, feeling they know better, dismisses her input. The team members, confident in their expertise, consider themselves to be the most knowledgeable of Sarah's father's needs and preferences. As a result, Sarah's contributions are undervalued, leading her to feel excluded and frustrated. The competitive atmosphere fosters feelings of inadequacy and a lack of trust between Sarah and the care staff, ultimately hindering effective care for her father.

I heard this over and over so have taken all of the stories and put them together…..Due to overwhelmed and restricted health and social systems, the triage to care means that only those who are in the "worst" situations receive services. This leads caregivers to believe that if they are not getting services it is because their situation is not "bad enough". This leads to feelings of inadequacy in their own skills and abilities to manage. This is made worse by little to no communication after completing copious amounts of detailed paperwork to try and obtain help. Families are left floundering. In order to "bolster" applications, caregivers are advised to focus on all of the worst aspects of the care needs and caregiver demands adding to the loss of hope and despair over their situation. This cycle not only exhausts their resources but erodes their sense of self-worth, as they are led to believe that their care needs don't matter. This competition for resources, created by the limitations of the system itself, adds unnecessary stress to an already difficult caregiving journey.

Recommendations for Family Caregivers:

- **Build Collaborative Relationships**: Foster an environment of teamwork rather than competition with other family members. Open, honest communication is key. Rather than viewing the care team as competition, focus on building collaborative relationships with professionals. Create space

for open dialogue where all parties — caregivers, professionals, and family members — can contribute to the care plan.
- **Set Boundaries**: Clearly define roles and responsibilities with other caregivers to avoid overstepping.
- **Focus on the Person's Needs**: Ensure the focus remains on the well-being of the person being cared for, not on who is doing more.
- **Create Clear Roles**: Establish clear caregiving roles with other family members to avoid confusion and prevent a sense of competition.
- **Communicate Needs**: Discuss openly what each person can realistically contribute to caregiving and how to balance tasks fairly.
- **Use a Shared Calendar**: Implement a shared online calendar or app where all caregivers can log their shifts, tasks, and appointments to ensure everyone is aligned.
- **Assert Your Expertise**: Stand firm in your knowledge of your loved one's needs. Make sure your voice is heard during care discussions and decisions. Share your experiences, concerns, and suggestions with the care team as a valuable partner in care.
- **Prioritize Your Role as a Caregiver**: Remind yourself of the importance of your role, even when professionals or institutions seem to undermine you. You are the expert in your loved one's life, and your input is invaluable.
- **Request Family Meetings**: Ask for regular meetings with care teams and institutions to ensure your voice is included in the care process. These meetings can help establish a shared understanding of roles and responsibilities.
- **Advocate**: Don't be afraid to advocate for your person because you are thinking or worrying about others. Advocating for you and your person is not advocating

against someone else. Identify what is yours to carry and leave the rest for those who have that responsibility.

Recommendations for Professionals:

- **Address Family Tensions**: If family conflict is evident, offer to mediate discussions to align their goals and encourage cooperation or refer them to a counsellor who specializes in family dynamics in caregiving situations.
- **Encourage Teamwork**: Promote a collaborative approach to caregiving, where everyone's strengths are acknowledged and utilized. Foster a culture of shared responsibility through regular check-ins with all caregivers involved or providing resources that help them feel equipped and confident.
- **Be Neutral**: Remain neutral in family dynamics, not favouring one caregiver over another, and offer support to all involved.
- **Encourage Family Collaboration**: Help families develop a care plan that incorporates everyone's skills and availability to prevent competition and confusion.
- **Acknowledge Diverse Strengths**: Recognize and encourage the unique contributions each family caregiver brings to the table, fostering an inclusive environment.
- **Recognize Family Caregivers as Equal Partners:** Actively involve caregivers in care discussions and decisions. Recognize that they bring valuable knowledge and experience to the table, and their perspective is just as important as your professional expertise.
- **Promote and Participate in Collaborative Care Models:** Create systems that encourage caregivers and professionals to work together as equal partners. This may involve joint care planning, regular check-ins, and open communication.

- **Avoid Role Confusion:** Professionals should refrain from acting as the "family" or "best friend" to the care recipient. Acknowledge that the family caregiver has the deepest, most sustained relationship with the person in care and must be treated as a key collaborator.
- **Provide Family Caregiver Support:** Offer caregivers resources, training, and support to empower them in their roles. Encourage their active participation in care planning and implementation.
- **Respect Boundaries**: Openness, honesty, and transparency are important but so are boundaries and professionalism. While caregivers may benefit from gaining an understanding of organizational and fiscal constraints, it can also cause moral distress, fear of advocating for themselves and their person, and a delay in advocating for and receiving services.
- **Advocate**: Continue to advocate for your clients, programs and services, and your organization. Equity and needs-based care versus competition for services can help reduce the moral distress, burnout, and decision-fatigue that professionals and caregivers are experiencing. Professionals and caregivers have the same goals and compassion and empathy for each other can reduce the blame and shame that can occur as we try to manage our own responses. Taking care of yourself helps you take care of others.

Recommendations for Organizations:

- **Facilitate Family Meetings**: Organize regular family meetings involving caregivers, healthcare professionals, and administrators to ensure that everyone is aligned and that caregivers' voices are heard, as part of care planning to ensure everyone is on the same page and can voice

concerns, to review the care plan, address concerns, and ensure that everyone's input is valued.
- **Provide Conflict Resolution Training**: Provide caregivers with conflict resolution tools and strategies to address family tensions before they escalate.
- **Support Caregiver Role Clarity**: In healthcare settings, ensure that roles and responsibilities are clearly outlined and that each caregiver is given the tools they need to succeed.
- **Encourage Shared Care**: Develop policies that encourage shared caregiving responsibilities, with organizations offering tools or resources for better collaboration.
- **Implement Family-Centred Care Models:** Develop and support care models that actively include caregivers in all decision-making processes. This includes ensuring caregivers' expertise and input are valued and integrated into the care plan.
- **Address Caregiver Concerns with Respect:** Ensure that caregivers' concerns are addressed in a timely and respectful manner. Create a system where caregivers can feel confident that their input will not be dismissed and that their role is appreciated.
- **Offer Respite and Resources:** Provide accessible respite care and resources for caregivers to help them manage their duties without feeling they must compete with others for support.
- **Keep Caregivers Updated**: This can be about wait lists, service and program changes, eligibility criteria, and other critical information for informed decision-making that extend beyond your organization. Not only do employees need this information to share with clients or potential clients but so do referring agencies, and those seeking services. Creating realistic expectations can reduce stress and anxiety for everyone.

- **Think Creatively**: There are many ways to solve challenges. Explore what is within the realm of possibility to manage the competition for scarce resources. This can be how services are offered, partnering with other organizations or providers, advocacy work, collaboration, share services, and more. Necessity is the mother of invention.

Recommendations for Policy Makers:

- **Provide Conflict Resolution Resources:** Fund programs that help resolve conflicts between caregivers and professionals, especially when competition for resources, attention, or authority arises. Provide readily accessible resources for conflict mediation in caregiving families to resolve disputes fairly and prevent burnout.
- **Support Mediation**: Fund and support family mediation programs that help resolve caregiving disputes in a constructive manner.
- **Support Family Care Team Approaches**: Design programs or policies that support teamwork among family caregivers, such as funding for family care teams or collaborative caregiving models.
- **Promote Shared Decision-Making**: Develop policies that encourage shared decision-making in care settings, so all caregivers feel as though they are equal partners and confident to contribute to care planning.
- **Support Collaborative Care Teams:** Design policies that encourage collaboration among family caregivers, healthcare providers, and organizations. Offer incentives for team-based care approaches where all parties contribute to the care plan.
- **Promote Family-Centred Care Policies:** Advocate for policies that ensure family caregivers are recognized as key

partners in care. This includes funding programs that support caregiver inclusion in decision-making processes and family-centred care models.
- **Ensure Fair Resource Allocation:** Develop policies that ensure caregivers have equal access to resources and support, regardless of their ability to advocate or "prove" their need. Ensure that funding allocations are needs based.
- **Include Caregivers in Co-Design and Co-Production**: Policies, programs and services must include caregivers as part of co-design and co-production models. Meaningful participation will ensure that the needs of caregivers are heard and part of the metrics for program and service success.

Key Takeaways:

1. **Equity is Essential to Quality Care**: Toxic competition may be fuelled by the professional systems that exclude or undervalue family caregivers. Whether in distribution of services or collaboration in care, equity is a fundamental value for service delivery.
2. **Caregivers are Care Partners**: Caregivers must assert their role and expertise, and work collaboratively with professionals to ensure a holistic and effective care plan. Professionals must actively involve caregivers in care decisions, value their unique contributions, and foster collaborative care models.
3. **Family-Centred Care is Holistic Care**: Organizations should adopt family-centred care practices and ensure caregivers are supported, respected, and included in all aspects of care.
4. **Co-Design and Co-Production Includes Caregivers**: Policymakers should create and implement policies, programs and services that promote fairness, collaboration, and resource access for caregivers, preventing toxic competition.

5. **Underfunding and Scarcity Results in Competition**: The competition over scarce resources will create moral distress, decision fatigue, and burnout — in staff and in caregivers. This then translates in higher system costs through staff turnover, caregiver health issues, and the utilization of more costly supports and services.

Summary:

Unhealthy competition in caregiving environments is a product not just of family dynamics, but of systems that marginalize caregivers' voices and undervalue their critical role. Professionals and organizations must recognize family caregivers as equal partners in the care process, ensuring that their insights and expertise are treated with the respect they deserve. Funders must support caregivers and the supports and services that they and their person rely on. Caregivers are the front line upon which the weight falls as they shield their person. By fostering a collaborative, supportive environment, we can reduce competition, improve outcomes, and provide caregivers with the resources and dignity they need to provide the best care possible.

Chapter 4: Lack of Recognition

"Caregiving can feel like a battle on all fronts: at home, with the person you care for, in the workplace (if you have one), and with the professionals and organizations that are supposed to provide assistance. But what happens when you are expected to care for a loved one, and in doing so, you sacrifice your own health, your emotional well-being, and your very identity? And when you turn to the very systems that should be supporting you, healthcare, social services, even your own family, what happens when they turn toxic, leaving you feeling more alone and more unsupported than ever?"

Recognition is a core element of human motivation, and for caregivers, it is a vital component of sustaining their well-being. When caregivers' hard work and sacrifices are continually overlooked, it leads to feelings of frustration, disengagement, and burnout. The systemic lack of recognition in the caregiving sphere further contributes to this problem. Caregivers often feel invisible, unsupported, and unappreciated, whether it's the neglect of recognition of their contributions by providers, the absence of societal recognition, or the failure of family members to offer tangible acknowledgment and support.

From the health and social services systems to societal policies, recognition of caregivers' labour and sacrifices is often missing. In fact, caregivers can often feel shoved aside and their perspectives only seen once validated by professionals. Research shows that for employees, "feeling respected" is one of the most powerful predictors of organizational success. The same applies to caregivers. When caregivers don't feel seen or appreciated, the overall caregiving process becomes less effective and far more exhausting. This chapter explores how the lack of recognition affects caregivers and provides strategies for caregivers, professionals, organizations, and policymakers to ensure that caregivers are properly valued.

Examples:

After months of caregiving, Mark, who provides care for his mother with Alzheimer's disease, is criticized when a doctor's appointment is missed due to a scheduling conflict. Although Mark handles many of his mother's daily needs, from medications to emotional support, his consistent dedication is overlooked when mistakes occur. The feedback he receives is harsh, with little recognition of the daily sacrifices he's made. The sacrifices he makes, like missing out on social events and personal time, go unnoticed. At times, his family members acknowledge how hard he's working but never offer him respite or tangible support. This lack of recognition leads to burnout and a sense of isolation for Mark.

Sarah, who cares for her father with chronic illness, spends hours advocating for her father's care in the hospital. However, during meetings with the medical team, her input is disregarded, and the focus is entirely on the team's perspective of the patient's needs.

Despite Sarah's significant involvement in managing her father's condition and day-to-day caregiving responsibilities, the care team fails to publicly acknowledge her contributions and provide her with the information and support she will need to continue to care for her father at hone. This lack of acknowledgment by the medical staff leaves Sarah feeling invisible and unappreciated.

Lisa, a family caregiver to her son with special needs, spends countless hours navigating the healthcare system, seeking out resources, completing paperwork, and advocating for her son's education and care. Yet, despite these significant efforts, her contributions are never acknowledged by the healthcare providers or the education system. She feels her role is reduced to an afterthought, and the emotional toll this takes on her is ignored by both institutions. If an agency was completing this work, they would be paid, while caregivers are specifically excluded from being able to receive any compensation.

Government policies fail to recognize the unpaid labour of family caregivers, even though they save the healthcare system millions by providing long-term care. Caregivers like Andrea, who sacrifices her career and personal well-being to care for her elderly mother, receive no financial support or compensation and shoulder the burden of many costs, including in their careers and therefore income and pension potential. The lack of tax breaks, stipends, or formal recognition from society leaves Andrea feeling undervalued and financially strained and with an uncertain future for herself.

Recommendations for Family Caregivers:

- **Celebrate Your Role and Efforts**: Recognize and celebrate your own efforts and value as a caregiver, even when no one else does. Take pride in your role and the progress you're making, no matter how small. Find small ways to celebrate your achievements, even if they aren't

immediately recognized by others. Acknowledging your own contribution is vital for preventing burnout.
- **Seek Validation from Others**: Talk to supportive friends, family, or mentors who understand the demands of caregiving. They can provide validation and help you navigate feelings of invisibility.
- **Advocate for Yourself**: It's okay to request recognition for your efforts. If you're feeling undervalued, talk with healthcare providers or other family members about how you'd like to be recognized for your efforts. Whether it's during family conversations or with healthcare providers, advocate for the recognition you deserve.
- **Track Your Contributions and Impact**: Keep a record of milestones, successful interventions, or positive changes in your loved one's condition. Share these with the caregiving team to highlight your role in the care process.
- **Seek Professional Support**: If you feel invisible or unrecognized, consider seeking professional support, such as a caregiver coach or therapist, to help you navigate these feelings.
- **Request Acknowledgment**: Don't hesitate to ask for recognition and respect for your input from healthcare teams or family members if you feel your contributions are being overlooked. Your contributions and perspectives are valuable and impact the care of your person in very significant ways. Advocate to be heard and the information you carry to be included in care planning.
- **Seek Peer Support**: Engage with other caregivers to share experiences and receive validation and acknowledgment from peers who understand your efforts. Support groups provide a space for shared experiences and mutual validation, where you can encourage each other.

Recommendations for Professionals:

- **Offer Emotional Support**: Many caregivers feel emotionally drained and under-appreciated. Providing emotional support through validation, reassurance, and positive feedback can help combat feelings of invisibility.
- **Offer Genuine Praise and Express Gratitude**: Regularly express appreciation for caregivers' efforts, dedication and hard work, whether through verbal praise or acknowledging their successes and importance of their role. Be specific in your appreciation. For example, "I see how hard you've worked to manage these medications, and it's making a real difference."
- **Treat Caregivers as Partners**: Recognize caregivers as essential members of the care team and encourage their input in care planning, ensuring that their insights are valued. Consider the information shared by caregivers with the same credibility as you would from other care team members.
- **Celebrate Caregiving Milestones**: Acknowledge significant caregiving milestones, such as improvements in the patient's health or major caregiving achievements, to show that you see and appreciate the caregiver's dedication and contributions to the success.
- **Offer Public Recognition**: Feature caregiver contributions in newsletters, care plan meetings, or community events, providing broader recognition for their essential role in patient care.
- **Acknowledge Caregiver Role in Patient/Client Safety**: As one of the lines of defence in patient safety, it can be caregivers who catch misinterpretations of information and documentation errors due to their global knowledge of treatments, services, and assessment data. As the central keeper of key patient history and current condition as well

as responses to treatments across service providers, they are frequently the ones to transfer knowledge throughout the continuum of their person's care.

Recommendations for Organizations:

- **Create Recognition Programs:** Establish formal programs that recognize caregivers for their hard work and dedication. This could include caregiver appreciation days, awards, or special acknowledgments in newsletters or meetings.
- **Incorporate Caregivers in Care Planning**: Involve caregivers in all aspects of the care process, ensuring they are recognized for their expertise and contribution to the patient's care plan. This is critical to support patient safety in transitions of care where evidence shows there are the most significant gaps and increased risk of errors.
- **Seek Meaningful Feedback**: Develop systems that allow caregivers to provide feedback about their experiences, showing that their voices are heard and valued.
- **Know Who Your Caregivers Are**: Along with the caregivers that your organization may interact with, you likely have caregivers as employees, and dual caregivers who serve as caregivers in their professionals and personal lives. Understanding who are caregivers and their needs can help you better understand your role(s) in working with and supporting caregivers. Wellness and burnout prevention programs benefit from being looked at through this lens. So do your programs and services that you offer clients/patients and their caregivers.
- **Create Support Groups**: Set up caregiver support groups where caregivers can meet and share their experiences, offering peer-based recognition and validation.

- **Provide Caregiver Benefits**: Develop programs that offer benefits or rewards for caregivers, such as discounts, access to wellness programs, or paid time off to acknowledge their sacrifices.
- **Establish Mentorship Programs**: Set up mentorship or coaching programs that allow experienced caregivers to mentor newer ones, recognizing their expertise and fostering a sense of accomplishment.
- **Support Caregivers in Their Role:** Offer resources, training, and groups for caregivers to ensure they feel competent and confident in their role. This type of support can also help mitigate the feeling of invisibility.

Recommendations for Policy Makers:

- **Fund Recognition Programs**: Provide funding to organizations that offer recognition programs for caregivers, such as "caregiver of the year" awards or public acknowledgment initiatives.
- **Offer Financial Recognition**: Support tax incentives, stipends, retirement savings options, reimbursement for caregiving-related expenses, and financial grants for caregivers who provide substantial care, acknowledging their contribution to the healthcare system.
- **Increase Public Awareness of Caregivers' Contributions:** Launch national campaigns to raise awareness about the importance of caregivers and the challenges they face. This can help shift public perception and promote greater recognition of caregivers.
- **Create a National Caregiver Recognition Week**: Create an official week dedicated to recognizing the contributions of family caregivers, providing a platform to celebrate and raise awareness of their hard work.

- **Develop Legal Protections**: Enact laws that provide job security, financial relief, and other protections for caregivers to recognize their role in the healthcare system and the balance between formal work and caregiving.

Key Takeaways:

1. **Recognition is Key:** Lack of recognition is a significant contributor to caregiver burnout and disengagement. Caregivers need acknowledgment from the health and social services systems and their friends and families.
2. **Self-Validation is Important:** Caregivers should recognize and celebrate their own contributions, even if others don't.
3. **Healthcare Professionals Should Acknowledge Caregivers:** Verbal praise, inclusion in decision-making, and emotional support are essential to making caregivers feel seen and valued.
4. **Organizations Should Establish Formal Recognition Programs:** Creating formal systems for recognizing caregivers can foster an environment of appreciation and support.
5. **Policy Makers Must Support Caregivers with Financial and Legal Recognition:** Financial incentives, legal protections, and public awareness campaigns can help caregivers feel valued and supported.
6. Caregivers Play a Key Role in Patient/Client Safety: As the people who know their person and the interactions with professionals and service providers best, caregivers play a key role in patient/client safety especially in transitions where the highest risk of errors exists.

Summary:

Recognition is not just a luxury for caregivers; it is essential to their well-being and the effectiveness of caregiving. Without acknowledgment, caregivers feel invisible and their vital contributions are undervalued. By fostering an environment of recognition, caregivers will feel more motivated, supported, and equipped to continue their important work. Whether through self-acknowledgment, support from professionals, organizational recognition, or policy-level change, caregivers deserve the recognition they've earned.

Chapter 5: Micromanagement

"Burnout is a canary in the coal mine. It's a warning sign of a toxic work environment. What we shouldn't do is question why the canary isn't tougher." Christina Maslach, PhD

Micromanagement in caregiving arises when family members, professionals, or even the person being cared for attempt to control or excessively supervise every aspect of caregiving. This lack of trust in the caregiver's capabilities and knowledge can undermine their confidence, increase stress, and strain relationships. Caregivers may feel as though their expertise and decisions are being constantly questioned or overruled, leading to frustration and a sense of helplessness.

Examples:

Even though Alice has been managing their mother's care for years and knows what works best, her siblings keep giving her detailed instructions on what to do and when. Alice's siblings also constantly question her decisions, such as how to assist with mobility or what foods to prepare, despite Alice's experience and training.

After Mary's hip surgery, a physical therapist insists on visiting at home multiple times to oversee the care plan, even though Ted,

Mary's husband and caregiver, has already been successfully following the instructions and managing well.

The discharge planner at the hospital micromanages the care team meetings, setting the agenda and giving Maureen's caregiver daughter Kim, little say or input, including when the meeting will occur. Kim's participation is limited, if she is invited at all. When Kim speaks up to provide input, she just gets stared at and then the discussion moves on as if she didn't say anything at all. The manager then determines the next steps and actions without seeking Kim's input and discussing the feasibility for Kim to manage it on top of everything else. When Kim tries to challenge their ideas they ignore her and proceed with their own plan of action.

Kathy, who is seen as "difficult" by staff and management of the group home her daughter lives in for advocating and speaking up regarding information and concerns, is required to sign an "agreement" limiting her ability to visit or communicate with staff regarding her daughter's care, even though she is the legal guardian. This adds emotional strain and disempowerment to Kathy's role and negatively impacts the relationship between Kathy and her daughter.

Jennifer is the parent of a child with developmental disabilities who is undergoing an assessment to determine skills and required supports into adulthood. Throughout the assessment, Jennifer is constantly questioned as to the accuracy and validity of her responses. She is asked to justify and explain every response. On those she isn't questioned it is because the professional also completing it agrees with her. She starts to doubt herself and becomes confused as to her own assessment of everything that she does for her daughter. She struggles between downplaying what she does, articulating her daughters strengths, and balancing what her daughter truly needs for support. Yet she knows that all future services are based on this assessment. She feels overwhelmed, exhausted, incompetent at being able to accurately articulate what her daughter requires, and comes away from it disillusioned by the process. Unless the required second person in the assessment validates her opinions then it is discounted and their opinion taken over hers.

Chantal, who is the primary caregiver of her father Andre, is subjected to constant check-ins by other family members, asking "Have you done it yet?" instead of offering help or solutions, leaving her feeling infantilized and unsupported.

Recommendations for Caregivers:

- **Set Boundaries**: If professionals or family members are micromanaging, calmly express your knowledge and experience in caring for your loved one. Communicate that you understand your loved one's needs and that your decisions should be respected. Set clear boundaries with professionals or family members who try to micromanage your caregiving decisions.
- **Be Assertive**: Advocate for your ability to make decisions and have autonomy over the caregiving process. Trust your experience and ensure that others understand that. Articulate your truth and don't let others make you second guess yourself.
- **Educate Others**: If someone is micromanaging, gently explain that you are well-versed in your loved one's needs and ask for specific guidance only when necessary. Educate others (family members or professionals) on the type of support you need and how they can help.
- **Request Autonomy**: Politely but firmly request the freedom to make caregiving decisions, especially if you have the knowledge and experience to do so.

- **Explain Your Expertise:** If someone attempts to micromanage, educate them about your familiarity with your loved one's needs. Accept specific guidance when needed, but make it clear you are capable of managing the caregiving tasks independently.

Recommendations for Professionals:

- **Trust Caregivers**: Acknowledge the wealth of knowledge caregivers possess. Trust them to make decisions and support them as partners in the caregiving process. Believe what they say versus constantly second guessing them or asking them to justify or prove their perspectives. Caregivers should feel like equal members of the care team and have a voice in decisions that affect their loved one's care.
- **Respect Caregivers and Their Role**: Provide guidance and resources, but avoid taking over decision-making. Caregivers should be allowed the space to manage the care plan without excessive interference. Trust that the caregiver knows their loved one best.
- **Promote and Participate in Collaborative Care**: Encourage team-based approaches that include the caregiver as an essential member of the care team.
- **Promote Caregiver Confidence**: Offer encouragement and positive reinforcement to build caregivers' confidence and reduce their need for micromanagement.
- **Build Trusting Relationships**: Micromanagement often stems from a lack of trust. Acknowledge that caregivers may have experienced previous traumas that led them to feel disempowered. Take steps to build trust through open communication, clear expectations, and respect for the caregiver's role.

Recommendations for Organizations:

- **Promote Autonomy in Care**: Treat caregivers as partners in care. Avoid creating systems that disempower caregivers or limit their autonomy in the care process.
- **Offer Caregiver Training**: Provide caregivers with the tools and knowledge they need to manage caregiving tasks effectively and feel confident in their caregiving and decisions.
- **Support Caregivers**: Develop systems that support caregiver autonomy while providing appropriate training and guidance to reduce unnecessary oversight.
- **Support Caregiver Leadership**: Encourage caregivers to take leadership roles in care, positioning professionals as advisors and collaborators rather than overseers. This fosters an environment of mutual respect and shared decision-making.
- **Minimize Bureaucracy**: Minimize red tape and administrative barriers that could result in unnecessary micromanagement. Streamline processes that allow caregivers to access support without frustration.
- **Assess Current Policies for "Caregiver-Friendliness"**: When policies are reviewed, there exists the opportunity to review them from a caregiver-friendly lens. Are caregivers part of co-design? Are they reflected in relevant polices of the organization? What changes could be made to better reflect caregiving?

Recommendations for Policy Makers:

- **Respect and Promote Caregiver Autonomy and Rights**: Craft policies that recognize caregivers as equal partners in care. Give caregivers the authority to make decisions without unnecessary oversight from professionals and undue interference.

- **Standardize Training for Caregivers**: Ensure that caregivers are provided with adequate training to feel confident in their caregiving role ensure they have the skills necessary to manage care effectively, reducing the need for micromanagement.
- **Standardize Training for Professionals**: Professionals should receive standardized training on the roles of caregivers, assessing caregiver needs, and developing and maintaining supportive relationships. This training should emphasize the importance of building trust and respecting caregivers as integral members of the care team.
- **Promote Family-Centred Care**: Promote and support policies that promote family-centred care models, where caregivers are treated as equal partners in care.

Key Takeaways:

1. **Recognition is Key**: The strengths, experience and knowledge of caregivers must be recognized and appreciated when providing guidance, support and resources. Caregivers need to be confident in their caregiving and feel valued, not undermined.
2. **Policy Matters**: Policies and policy language should reflect the status of caregivers as partners in care. This then signals the culture and norms of the organization as to how caregivers are included and treated within the organization and by the professionals within it.
3. **Build Trusting Relationships**: Trust needs to go both ways. When it is broken through behaviours such as micromanagement, the whole relationship is damaged. This can lead to errors and compromised care whereas trusting relationships improve quality and safety for the person being cared for.

4. **Caregivers as Partners**: By actively collaborating with caregivers as equal partners, their strengths and capabilities will be more readily seen and utilized to the benefit of everyone.
5. **Caregivers Know "Different"**: Not better, not less, just different. Just as we respect the roles, knowledge, and skills of other care team members, we need to respect that of caregivers. Harnessing their strengths for the good of the person needing care benefits everyone. Recognizing and appreciating their learning needs will make them stronger. Teach them what they need to know so they can continue to walk the path with their person throughout the day-to-day between professional contacts.

Summary:

When caregiver strengths, knowledge, skills and experience are acknowledged and appreciated, caregivers can thrive in their role. Professionals can play a pivotal role in supporting caregivers by providing guidance, resources and advice while building trusting relationships and respecting caregiver decisions. Policy and organizational structures need to provide a framework for collaborative care where caregivers are equal partners in care.

Chapter 6: Favouritism and Discrimination

"What boggles my mind is that as his wife and caregiver, I know him best. I attend all of the appointments and provide care. But they rarely include me in meetings or listen to my thoughts and ideas. Why don't they listen to me?"

In caregiving dynamics, favouritism and discrimination can significantly impact family relationships and the quality of care. When certain family members are favoured, it can lead to feelings of resentment and burnout for others. Additionally, bias from professionals can exacerbate the issue, leaving some caregivers feeling overlooked, undervalued, or excluded from important decisions. These situations often arise from complex family dynamics, societal expectations, or implicit biases. Addressing favouritism and discrimination requires open communication, a commitment to fairness, and intentional support for all caregivers involved.

Examples:

Amy is expected to take on most of the caregiving duties for her aging parents because she's local, while her siblings (who live farther away) are rarely asked to help, even though they have the means to do so. Although she lives nearby and manages most of her mother's care, her brother, Mark, who lives far away, is always praised for "being there" for their mom. Amy handles daily tasks like appointments, medications, and physical assistance, but no one acknowledges the sheer amount of work she does. Mark's occasional phone calls are given the spotlight, leaving Amy feeling under-appreciated and overwhelmed.

Alicia is a nurse and also a caregiver for her daughter with multiple health conditions. When interacting with members of her daughter's care team, Alicia feels she is being "othered" as she is not seen as being knowledgeable. She is labelled as caregiver and not seen as also being a professional. This leads to information not being shared with her or not being invited to critical appointments or meetings. Also, Alicia is made to run around to get more written information from "professionals" to share with the other team members as she, as the caregiver providing the information, is deemed insufficient or untrustworthy. Only "objective professional opinions" are deemed valid.

Linda, a dedicated daughter, has been caring for her elderly mother for years. However, when interacting with healthcare providers, Linda finds that her husband, Dave, is often treated as the primary decision-maker, simply because of his gender. Though Linda has been providing most of the care, her opinions are dismissed, and Dave's decisions are prioritized. This leaves Linda feeling sidelined, despite her intimate knowledge of her mother's needs.

Recommendations for Family Caregivers:

- **Speak Up for Fairness**: It's crucial to have open conversations with family members when you feel like caregiving duties are unfairly distributed. If you feel overwhelmed while others aren't contributing equally, have a respectful discussion to make sure everyone shares the load. For example, try saying, *"I'm handling a lot of the* *day-to-day care, and I could really use more help. Can we figure out a way to share responsibilities?"*

- **Collaborate to Promote Equity**: Working together as a team can reduce feelings of resentment. Make caregiving tasks clear and agreed upon. For example, create a shared schedule to ensure everyone knows what tasks they're responsible for. This will make it harder for anyone to be left out or overlooked, especially when multiple people are involved.
- **Be Clear About and Set Expectations**: Make sure roles and responsibilities are clear and agreed upon to avoid misunderstandings. Sometimes family members expect things to be done a certain way without discussing it. To avoid frustration, set expectations from the start. For instance, instead of assuming someone knows they need to help on weekends, say, "I need you to help with Dad's care every Saturday from 2 to 4 PM. Is that something you can commit to?"
- **Keep a Written Record of Caregiving Tasks**: If you notice ongoing inequities, document the caregiving responsibilities you've taken on. Having a clear record will help you communicate effectively with your family about the imbalance. For example, jot down dates and duties you've covered and bring this up during discussions about workload distribution. Create a shared calendar of tasks clearly marking who is taking responsibility for them.
- **Seek External Support**: If the situation feels impossible to handle alone, seek help from a neutral third party, like a family counsellor or caregiver support group. They can help facilitate difficult conversations and ensure everyone feels heard and treated fairly.
- **Articulate Your Knowledge and Expertise**: Beyond what you know as a caregiver and someone with uniques knowledge of your person, you are also a full person with

your own training, knowledge, skills, and expertise that you bring to your caregiving role. All of this is valuable and should be valued and respected. Speak up and share what you know and the perspectives with which you bring forth that information.

Recommendations for Professionals:

- **Treat All Caregivers Equally**: As a professional, it's vital to offer equal attention to all caregivers, regardless of gender, financial resources, or assertiveness. Recognize and acknowledge the efforts of quieter or less financially affluent caregivers who may be doing the bulk of the caregiving. Make sure everyone feels valued and heard.
- **Promote Inclusivity**: Ensure that all caregivers have access to the same resources, information, and support.
- **Monitor for Bias and Address It**: Be mindful of biases, whether based on gender, age, or social status. Ensure that all caregivers, regardless of their background, receive equal attention, respect, and recognition. If you observe biased behaviour or preferential treatment, speak up and correct it promptly.
- **Promote Equal Access to Resources**: Every caregiver should have access to the same resources and information. For example, make sure that all family caregivers are aware of available financial assistance, caregiving tools, and professional support, regardless of their financial or social standing.
- **Facilitate Open Communication Among Caregivers**: When tensions arise within families, help caregivers navigate communication. Facilitate conversations to ensure everyone has a chance to voice their concerns, feelings, and suggestions. For instance, if one family member feels left

out of caregiving decisions, encourage a family meeting to discuss how everyone can be more involved and informed.
- **Refer to Mediation Services**: If favouritism or discrimination is ongoing, refer the family to professional mediation services or family counselling to resolve conflicts impartially.
- **Respect Caregivers as the Person They Are**: We are all the sum of our parts. Caregivers also have other background, knowledge, skills, training, expertise, that benefit their person and enhance the care team for their person. Meet caregivers where they are at and recognize the diversity amongst various caregivers.

Recommendations for Organizations:

- **Ensure Equal Access to Caregiving Resources**: Make sure that all caregivers have access to the same resources and support, no matter their background or financial situation. For instance, offer equal access to training, support groups, and caregiving tools for all family members involved in the care process.
- **Offer Bias Training for Caregivers and Staff**: Organize training for staff to recognize and mitigate biases that could influence caregiving support. This will help ensure that all family members are treated equally and that caregiving decisions are based on need, not implicit biases.
- **Create Inclusive Policies**: Implement clear policies against discrimination, favouritism, and bias within caregiving teams, ensuring that all caregivers feel equally supported.
- **Promote Family Engagement**: Encourage organizations to involve all caregivers equally in care planning and decision-making processes, ensuring transparency.

- **Cultural Competency Training**: Provide training for staff on recognizing and mitigating discrimination or bias in caregiving situations, particularly in diverse families.
- **Offer Dispute Resolution Services**: Offer conflict resolution programs to help caregivers resolve disagreements and ensure fairness in caregiving duties.
- **Promote Collaborative Care Planning:**
  Encourage collaborative caregiving, where everyone's voice is heard. Caregiving plans should be developed with input from all involved family members, and everyone should feel equally involved in decision-making.
- **Recognize Caregiver Diversity**: Any caregiver-related programs or policies should recognize and appreciate the diversity of caregivers. They are not a homogenous group. Meeting each caregiver where they are at and propelling them forward supports patients/clients, professionals, and organizations though person-centred practices.

Recommendations for Policy Makers:

- **Make Inclusive Policies the Norm**: Create and enforce policies that ensure all caregivers are treated equally and have access to the same support, regardless of gender, race, or socio-economic status.
- **Enforce Anti-Discrimination Laws**: Introduce or strengthen laws that protect caregivers from discrimination, ensuring that they have equal rights and access to resources, regardless of background, gender, race, financial situation, or relationship to the patient. This could include equal access to caregiving benefits and protection from bias in the workplace or healthcare settings.
- **Support Family Caregiver Rights**: Create policies that explicitly protect family caregivers from unfair treatment

and ensure equal access to caregiving resources and benefits.
- **Enhance Workplace Protections**: Establish stronger workplace protections for caregivers to ensure they're not penalized or discriminated against in employment due to caregiving responsibilities. Support the creation and sustainability of caregiver-friendly workplaces.
- **Implement Data Collection and Monitoring**: Implement programs to collect data on discrimination or favouritism in caregiving settings to better understand and address the issue.
- **Support Policies That Foster Family-Centred Care:** Create policies that emphasize family-centred care, where all caregivers—whether male, female, wealthy, or not—are treated as equal partners in the caregiving process. These policies should promote collaboration, respect, and shared responsibility.
- **Strengthen Financial and Legal Support for Caregivers:** Support policies that provide financial assistance or legal protections for family caregivers. Ensure that everyone, regardless of income or social background, has access to support systems like respite care, financial benefits, and training resources.

Key Takeaways:

1. **Family Caregiving Dynamics:** Favouritism can emerge when caregiving duties are unevenly distributed, with certain family members expected to do more because of gender, proximity, or implicit biases.
2. **Professional Bias:** Professionals may unintentionally show favouritism, giving more attention to caregivers with stronger financial resources, louder voices, or certain gender roles.

3. **Impact on Caregivers:** Caregivers who feel discriminated against or left out can experience stress, burnout, and frustration, affecting both their well-being and their caregiving effectiveness.
4. **Steps for Change:** Advocating for fairness, improving communication, and ensuring equal access to resources are key ways to combat favouritism and discrimination in caregiving settings.

Summary:

Favouritism and discrimination in caregiving scenarios can lead to frustration, burnout, and a lack of collaboration between caregivers. Whether it's based on gender, financial resources, or implicit biases, it's crucial for families, professionals, and organizations to recognize and address these issues. Open communication, equal access to resources, and clear expectations are essential for creating a more equitable caregiving environment. By fostering fairness and treating all caregivers with respect, we can help ensure that caregiving is a shared responsibility that strengthens relationships, reduces stress, and enhances the care provided to loved ones.

Chapter 7: Toxic Leadership

"What do you do when the person you care for is toxic? When love becomes manipulation, and duty becomes resentment? What happens when the caregiving relationship itself is the source of your pain?"

Toxic leadership isn't confined to the workplace. It can also emerge within caregiving relationships, where a loved one, such as a parent or relative, manipulates or emotionally harms the caregiver. This toxic behaviour can take many forms: guilt-tripping, verbal abuse, unreasonable expectations, or dismissiveness. A caregiver may feel trapped, unable to stand up for themselves, all while facing an overwhelming burden of care. This manipulation is not limited to family members; some healthcare professionals or social service leaders may adopt toxic leadership traits as well, exhibiting behaviours like emotional neglect, disrespect, or even gaslighting caregivers, making them question their role and needs. Further, professionals may disagree with decisions made by the caregiver on behalf of their loved one and attempt to manipulate or pressure caregivers to make decisions that are more aligned with their beliefs. Organizational leadership may also perpetuate toxic dynamics by showing bias or having negative beliefs about caregivers, especially those who are navigating difficult decisions, such as placing their loved ones in care. These issues can strain the caregiving experience and add significant emotional and physical stress.

Examples:

Clara, a devoted daughter, feels torn between caring for her aging mother and living her own life. Her mother constantly guilt-trips her, saying things like, "You don't love me enough to take care of me," whenever Clara takes a break or sets a boundary. The emotional manipulation eats away at Clara, and she begins to feel like she's failing, even though she's doing her best. This leaves her feeling exhausted, isolated, and resentful.

Sophia is overwhelmed by the care her grandmother needs and raises concerns with the case manager. The response is dismissive, suggesting that Sophia "doesn't understand" her grandmother's medical condition. The case manager's lack of empathy and understanding makes Sophia feel incompetent, even though she's the one providing daily hands-on care. The social worker at the hospital pressures Sophia to accept a care option (such as moving her grandmother to a facility) without providing adequate support or alternatives, making Sophia feel like she has no choice.

Cheryl is frustrated by the isolation from other parents of the children that live in her daughter's group home. The organization uses "confidentiality" as the rationale to prevent the parents from connecting with each other, leaving them isolated and unsupported. When it comes to organizational activities like fundraisers or other initiatives, however, confidentiality seems to be thrown out the window, reinforcing caregivers' dependence on the organization and exacerbating their feelings of isolation.

"What if your boss was someone you loved deeply? What if the emotional manipulation, unrealistic expectations, and burnout were coming from the

person you care for, not a colleague or supervisor? What if 'toxic leadership' wasn't limited to the workplace, but something you dealt with at home every day?"

Recommendations for Family Caregivers:

- **Speak Up and Assert Yourself**: If you feel that a professional is being toxic or manipulative, express your concerns calmly and assertively. If you feel that a family member or healthcare professional is being manipulative or toxic, it's important to express your concerns calmly but assertively. For example, if your loved one is guilt-tripping you, say, *"I understand that you need me, but I also need time to recharge. I can't be at my best without rest."*
- **Document Interactions**: Keep a record of any toxic or manipulative behaviour, whether it's from a family member, a healthcare professional or leadership. Write down the dates, what was said or done, and how it made you feel. This documentation can be crucial if you need to address the issue later with a third party or seek support.
- **Know Your Rights as a Caregiver**: You have the right to advocate for yourself and your loved one. Understand what rights you have as a caregiver and patient advocate so that you can stand firm when facing toxic leadership or behaviour. For example, familiarize yourself with laws or guidelines that protect caregivers from emotional abuse or unfair treatment. Keep documentation regarding complaint and dispute resolution processes in a place you can find them easily if you feel you need them.
- **Set Clear Boundaries**: Toxic leadership often thrives in environments where boundaries aren't respected. Whether it's a family member, provider, or even an organization, set clear boundaries about what is and isn't acceptable. For

instance, if a provider is being dismissive, you might say, *"I need you to listen to my concerns and provide answers, not dismiss them. This is important for my loved one's care."*

- **Seek Mediation and Support from Allies**: If you feel unsupported or isolated, seek out allies. Whether it's other family members or support groups, you don't have to face toxic leadership alone. A neutral third-party mediator, lawyer, or advocate can help facilitate difficult conversations within families, ensuring that everyone's voice is heard and respected.

Recommendations for Professionals:

- **Model Positive Leadership**: Healthcare professionals should lead by example, showing empathy, respect, and professionalism when interacting with family caregivers. For example, if a caregiver is overwhelmed, offer reassurance and suggestions for self-care instead of minimizing their concerns.
- **Be Transparent and Honest**: Avoid any perception of manipulative behaviour or hidden agendas. Always be open and forthcoming with caregivers about care plans, decision-making, and the reasoning behind your recommendations. If a caregiver has concerns, address them directly and provide clear, understandable responses.
- **Support Caregivers as Equal Team Members**: Offer encouragement to caregivers, so they feel competent and supported in their roles. For instance, if a caregiver is struggling with a particular aspect of care, offer specific advice or resources to help them learn and gain expertise.
- **Lead with Empathy**: Adopt a leadership style that is collaborative, empathetic, and supportive. Encourage

caregivers to express their concerns, and address issues in a timely, transparent manner.
- **Create Supportive Environments**: Professionals should create spaces where caregivers feel safe to voice their concerns and ask questions. Foster an environment where caregivers know they will be treated with respect, not experience fear of retaliation or criticism. Make sure caregivers are not made to feel guilty or incompetent for seeking respite or taking breaks.
- **Offer Constructive Feedback**: If caregivers are making mistakes or need more information and guidance, offer constructive feedback in a way that encourages growth rather than undermining their confidence or abilities.
- **Offer Resources for Self-Advocacy**: Provide caregivers with tools and information to help them advocate for themselves. This can include information on their rights, local caregiver support groups, and tips for setting boundaries with toxic individuals or professionals.

"When supports and services aren't enough and you are faced with putting your child with autism and aggression into a group home, you hope that there will finally be support, that you can focus on having a better relationship with your child. You never expect that the system, workers, group home owners and even the social service gatekeepers will treat you like you have abandoned your child. In fact, they make you say it if you want a placement and can't afford to pay the fees yourself. I begged for help and didn't get enough. I was all alone. In the group home my son has two staff at all times. Now that I am completely burnt out and have no

options, I am vilified for it. You think the battles are going to end but instead you are faced with a whole different set of battles."

Recommendations for Organizations:

- **Foster Positive Leadership**: Develop leadership programs that focus on positive, supportive leadership styles in caregiving settings. Teach staff to recognize toxic behaviours, both in themselves and others, the impact these behaviours can have on caregivers, and corrective actions they can take.
- **Cultivate a Supportive Culture**: Create a culture within your organization that values caregivers and ensures they feel heard, supported, and respected. This could involve regular caregiver check-ins, offering feedback channels, and ensuring staff treat caregivers with empathy and understanding.
- **Create a Space of Psychological Safety for Caregivers**: Establish environments where caregivers can connect with one another without fear of judgment or isolation. Encourage peer support groups, mentorship, and caregiver-led initiatives that foster a sense of community.
- **Acknowledge and Address the Power Dynamics**: There is an inherent power dynamic between leadership, professionals, employees, patients and caregivers. This power dynamic must be met with compassion and empathy and a commitment to collaboration. Treating caregivers as partners in care is one way that caregiver voices can be heard and their contributions valued and for this dynamic to be shifted. Family-centred care is another way that caregivers and their needs can be seen and met.

- **Implement Feedback Systems**: Create regular feedback systems that allow caregivers to report toxic leadership or other negative behaviours without fear of retaliation.
- **Provide Conflict Resolution Resources**: Ensure that conflict resolution processes are in place to address toxic leadership behaviours within caregiving organizations. Caregivers should know there is a clear, fair process they can rely on if they encounter toxic dynamics or leadership failures.
- **Implement Feedback and Accountability Systems:** Organizations should develop feedback systems that allow caregivers to report toxic behaviours or leadership issues without fear of retaliation. Ensure that these concerns are taken seriously and addressed promptly.

Recommendations for Policy Makers:

- **Hold Providers Accountable for Toxic Leadership:** Establish accountability measures for providers and organizations, ensuring that any toxic behaviour from staff toward caregivers is identified and addressed. This includes policies for reporting and handling complaints about manipulative or dismissive behaviour.
- **Implement Leadership Standards:** Set clear standards for leadership within healthcare and social service organizations, ensuring that leaders demonstrate professionalism, respect, and empathy. Toxic behaviour should not be tolerated, and leaders should be held to high standards of emotional intelligence and care.
- **Legislate Leadership Standards**: Implement and enforce standards for leadership behaviour in caregiving environments to ensure that leaders are trained to foster healthy, supportive work environments.

- **Enforce Anti-Retaliation Policies:** Make sure that caregivers who speak out against toxic leadership are protected from retaliation. This includes creating policies that safeguard caregivers from being punished for raising concerns or advocating for better treatment.
- **Support Leadership Training Programs:** Fund programs aimed at developing effective leadership in caregiving and healthcare settings. These programs should emphasize emotional intelligence, empathy, and the importance of supporting family caregivers.

Key Takeaways:

1. Toxic leadership in caregiving environments can manifest in emotional manipulation, dismissiveness, or micromanagement, often causing burnout and resentment in caregivers.
2. Family caregivers may face guilt-tripping or unrealistic expectations from loved ones, making it difficult to set boundaries or take care of themselves.
3. Professionals and organizations play a critical role in modelling positive leadership, fostering supportive environments, and offering resources for caregivers.
4. Caregivers can protect themselves by setting clear boundaries, documenting toxic behaviour, and seeking allies or third-party mediation when necessary.
5. Policy makers should establish clear standards for leadership in caregiving environments and enforce anti-retaliation policies to protect caregivers from toxic dynamics.

Summary:

Toxic leadership in caregiving environments can be just as damaging as in the workplace. Whether it's emotional manipulation by a loved one, dismissiveness from healthcare professionals, or a lack of support from organizational leadership, toxic dynamics can lead to burnout, resentment, and isolation. Addressing these toxic behaviours requires a proactive approach, including setting clear boundaries, fostering transparency, and creating supportive environments where caregivers feel respected. By advocating for themselves, seeking support, and promoting positive leadership, caregivers can reduce the impact of toxic leadership and improve their caregiving experience.

Chapter 8: High Levels of Stress and Burnout

"You love them, but you're exhausted. You're committed, but you're burned out. You give, but you're empty. This isn't just caregiving. This is survival in a toxic world that doesn't understand you."

Caregiving is often portrayed as an act of love, devotion, and selflessness. Caregiving is also inherently stressful, but when expectations exceed a caregiver's capacity without adequate respite, it leads to physical and emotional exhaustion. The stress and responsibility of caregiving, especially when it's relentless, leads to physical and emotional burnout, which can affect the caregiver's well-being. But what happens when that care starts to feel like a battle, a never-ending war between the responsibilities, and the caregiver's own health, and emotional well-being? When loving someone deeply and caring for them means being utterly exhausted, burned out, and emotionally depleted, it's not just about giving, it's about surviving. And while the world expects them to keep going, where is the support for the caregiver? How can they keep caring for others when the systems that should support them leave them feeling more alone and exhausted than ever? The systemic pressures within the healthcare system, or lack of adequate support services, can exacerbate caregiver burnout and stress. This chapter is a dive into the overwhelming stress, the toll that burnout takes, and how to navigate a path through it, before it consumes the caregiver completely.

Examples:

Sara is a caregiver for her aging mother with dementia. Sara manages a full-time job, balances a household, and juggles her mother's appointments, medication, and emotional needs. Over time, her days have grown longer and her nights shorter. She's constantly running on fumes, feeling physically and mentally drained. But the stress doesn't stop there. Sara's work demands are growing, her coworkers don't understand her situation, and the healthcare professionals overseeing her mother's care are distant and dismissive. One evening, after staying up late to resolve an insurance claim, Sara collapses from exhaustion. Her body aches, her mind foggy, and yet, there is no option to pause. The weight of caregiving, coupled with the lack of systemic support, pushes Sara closer to burnout.

David is a father, husband, and full-time caregiver for his wife, Linda, who has been living with chronic illness with increasingly frequent exacerbations for over two years. Between managing Linda's medical needs, handling household chores, and running his own business, David feels like he's sinking. He hasn't had a real break in months. When he tries to take a breather, he feels an overwhelming guilt that he's not doing enough. The pressure from work, home, healthcare, and even his own emotions, builds up. A month into this cycle, David experiences severe back pain from the constant physical strain. But even in this pain, the supports and services are inconsistent and still leave him providing much of the care.

Tammy, a caregiver for her son with multiple disabilities, feels completely overwhelmed and emotionally exhausted but continues to push through because she doesn't have the resources or support to take a break. The respite she can get only allows her to catch up on some of the things she can't get done when her son is with her. Due to her inability to work many hours, and the lack of any spousal or child support from her ex-husband, she is strained financially. This means that she can't afford to pay for additional help, if she could find it.

Sally, who is in her 70s and caring for her elderly mother, begins experiencing physical symptoms like headaches, fatigue, and weight loss due to the stress of caregiving. She is worried about her health and the possibility of an underlying medical condition but she has challenges finding time to make an appointment with her physician and getting someone to care for her mother so she can go.

Mandy has a full time job and manages caregiving duties. While services are available for part of her working hours, there is tremendous time and effort, as well as expense to get it all covered. Mandy frequently needs to flex her hours, missing lunch and making up time at night in order to meet the demands. When staff fail to show up or make time changes at the last minute, there is chaos for Mandy, causing her to miss work, lose pay and putting her job in jeopardy. This added fear and stress affects Mandy's sleep and mood, further adding to the overall strain. When replacement staff who do not know the client are sent, Mandy either ends up training the new person or doing it herself when the staff person is uncomfortable or unable to do the tasks required.

Reggie, who cared for both of his parents until his father passed away, continues to care for his mother who now has dementia. His parents have always been adamant about not going into a long-term care home so he has struggled to accommodate their wishes. The dementia symptoms are becoming too much for him to handle along with his own health issues, work, and maintaining everything else. This dilemma causes moral distress as he is faced with the difficult decision of considering having his northern placed in a home. He doesn't know what else to do but he doesn't want to fail his mother who always took such great care of and supported him.

> *"We call them 'family responsibilities,' but no one ever tells you that responsibility comes with a cost —one that can bankrupt your health, your peace of mind, and your future."*

Recommendations for Family Caregivers:

- **Continue to Practice Radical Hope**: "Holding on to radical hope means believing fiercely in the possibility of better days, even when standing in the middle of the storm." (Author Unknown). In the darkest moments, holding onto hope is vital. Radical hope isn't about ignoring the difficulty of the situation but about finding belief in the possibility of better days. Radical hope can help us recover from challenges and setbacks, inspire us to act and keep moving forward, and can balance realism and optimism. You will have hard days. I have had days where the best thing I could come up with in my daily bedtime gratitude thought was that the day was over, I could sleep, and when I wake up, it will be a new day, one which can be better than this one.
- **Prioritize Restorative Care**: Make caring for yourself, in a way that works for you, a priority. Restorative care may not mean bubble baths and massages. Establish routines that focus on your own health and well-being. Regular physical exercise, maintaining hobbies, taking a walk, or simply laughing with your person can make a huge difference.
- **Practice Self-Compassion**: It's ok to not know everything. It's ok to be doing the best you can with the knowledge and

capacity that you have - even if others have different opinions (they aren't in the same situation, the same circumstances, within which to try and make a decision). It's ok to not know what you need or want when someone asks you (because that may not have happened before and you haven't really stopped to think about you). It is ok to think that the help being offered is not what you need nor what you want and in fact may be disruptive instead of helpful. Give yourself some grace and know that you are doing what you can. Even if sometimes it is not your "best". Nobody is 100% all the time. Forgive yourself for these perceived and real things.

- **Delegate When Possible:** You don't have to carry the entire weight of caregiving alone. Ask for help from family, friends, or professionals. Delegating tasks, even small ones, can alleviate the pressure.
- **Seek Professional Support:** If the stress of caregiving becomes overwhelming, seek counselling or support groups for caregivers. Speaking to someone who understands the unique challenges can be a huge relief. This is particularly important when you are faced with difficult decisions or circumstances that are not well aligned with your, or your person's, beliefs.
- **Practice Stress-Reduction Techniques**: Incorporate stress-reduction practices into your daily routine, such as deep breathing exercises, mindfulness, yoga, or meditation.
- **Accept Help**: Ask for help from other family members, friends, or hired caregivers to relieve some of the pressure and prevent exhaustion.
- **Set Realistic Expectations**: Understand that you can't do everything. Set achievable goals each day and allow yourself to acknowledge that your best might look different from day to day, and that's okay.

Recommendations for Professionals:

- **Offer Emotional and Mental Health Support**: Acknowledge the emotional strain that caregivers are under and offer resources for coping, such as counselling, stress management classes, and support groups.
- **Monitor for Burnout**: Actively look for signs of caregiver burnout during appointments and intervene early if necessary.
- **Offer Respite Options**: Ensure caregivers know about respite care services. Encourage them to take breaks so they can recharge, as burnout is a serious issue that can impact caregiving quality.
- **Acknowledge Caregiver Stress**: Don't overlook the strain caregivers are under. Proactively ask about their well-being during appointments and offer guidance on how to manage stress.
- **Encourage Regular Breaks**: Recommend respite care and other ways for caregivers to take breaks and recharge, whether through short-term care options or support programs.
- **Validate Their Efforts**: Regularly acknowledge the hard work caregivers are doing and ensure they feel appreciated for their efforts.
- **Provide Education and Resources:** Equip caregivers with the knowledge they need to navigate the caregiving journey, from managing medical tasks to handling financial responsibilities.
- **Support Caregivers Through Making Difficult Decisions**: Sometimes the best and only decision to be made can be made more challenging by conflicting beliefs and values. This misalignment can create moral distress. If repeated decisions and circumstances create distress, it can harden into moral injury. This can then lead to burnout. By

providing support to caregivers through these decisions, the feelings of guilt, blame, and shame can be lessened. Compassion, empathy, space and grace are the antidote.

"Micro-stresses - that exhausted feeling is the culmination of micro-stresses. All the little things that drain our time and energy and wear us down, draining our capacity, depleting our emotional and physical reserves, chipping away at our ability to think, make decisions, stay motivated and be productive and challenge our identity and values."

Recommendations for Organizations:

- **Offer Caregiver Support Programs**: Develop or partner with organizations that offer support groups, counselling, and respite care to alleviate caregiver stress.
- **Develop Respite Care Programs**: Establish or partner with respite care services to give caregivers scheduled breaks. It's vital that caregivers have time to step away, even briefly, to maintain their own health.
- **Promote Work-Life Balance**: If you employ caregivers, offer policies that promote a healthy work-life balance, such as flexible hours, caregiving leave, or the option to work from home to reduce stress and burnout.
- **Offer Employee Assistance Programs**: Set up programs that offer mental health support, caregiver resources, and counselling services specifically for employees who are also caregivers.
- **Foster a Supportive Work Culture**: Encourage a culture of support and compassion within organizations, where caregivers feel comfortable discussing their needs and seeking assistance without fear of judgment or retaliation.

Recommendations for Policy Makers:

- **Implement Paid Family Leave**: Implement, enhance and expand paid family leave policies to reduce financial pressures and allow caregivers to take time off work without financial penalty, helping them manage stress and prevent burnout. Caregivers shouldn't have to choose between their loved one's care and their own financial stability.
- **Provide Financial Assistance**: Introduce financial relief through subsidies or tax credits for caregivers to ease the burden of unpaid labor and help them manage the costs associated with caregiving.
- **Fund Mental Health Services**: Increase funding for mental health services that are specifically geared towards caregivers, such as therapy, counselling, or caregiver stress relief programs.
- **Support Public Health Campaigns**: Launch public health campaigns that raise awareness of caregiver burnout, provide resources for managing stress, and highlight the importance of seeking help when needed. Educating the public can lead to better community support for caregivers.

Key Takeaways:

1. **Caregiving is Work:** Caregiving is a marathon, not a sprint. Burnout happens when caregivers push themselves too hard without proper support or respite.
2. **Caregivers Need Support to Practice Restorative Care:** Practicing self-compassion and setting realistic goals can help caregivers navigate the overwhelming stress. Supports and services that provide respite and opportunities are needed earlier to prevent burnout and keep caregivers healthy.

3. **Check in on Caregivers:** Professionals should actively recognize caregiver stress and provide both emotional and practical support.
4. **Caregivers Are Also Employees:** Organizations can support employees who are caregivers through flexible work options, mental health resources, and respite care programs.
5. **Government Policy Needs to Change:** Policymakers must create policies that provide financial relief, paid family leave, and increase access to caregiver-specific support services. Without caregivers, our health and social services systems would collapse.

Summary:

Caregiving can be incredibly rewarding, but it is also exhausting, emotionally draining, and physically demanding. The stress and burnout that caregivers experience often go unnoticed or unaddressed, especially when there are systemic gaps in support. Caregivers must find ways to prioritize their own well-being, set realistic goals, and reach out for help when needed. At the same time, professionals, organizations, and policymakers must step up to provide the necessary resources, mental health support, and flexibility to help caregivers cope with the overwhelming responsibilities they face. By implementing the right strategies and supports, we can ensure that caregivers not only survive, but thrive, in their vital roles.

Chapter 9: Lack of Work-Life Balance

"Sure. I'll just 'do yoga.' I'll find a class close by to minimize travel time and therefore costs of a respite worker (unless they have a minimum hours of duty); at a time when a worker is available; arrange to have a worker; get them set up for their shift and debrief afterwards; miss the class due to a cancellation or because the replacement doesn't know my loved one; and, on and on. The time, effort, and stress to 'do yoga' far exceeds any benefit that I would get out of a one-hour class. So even the things I want to do to help myself get taken away from me."

Caregiving is often referred to as a labour of love, but for many, it becomes an all-consuming responsibility that leaves little room for anything else. Imagine trying to carve out time for yourself in the midst of a chaotic caregiving schedule. You plan to attend an exercise class, hoping to find a sliver of peace in an otherwise overwhelming day. But by the time you arrange for a caregiver to take over, deal with cancellations, and manage all the logistics, the class feels like a distant dream rather than a moment of relaxation. And then, after all that, the worker cancels as you are getting ready to go out. This scenario is all too familiar for caregivers who struggle to balance their own needs with the demands of those they care for. When work and caregiving demands collide, personal time and well-being are often the first casualties. This chapter explores the painful reality of a lack of work-life balance for caregivers and how to reclaim space for oneself without guilt or stress.

Examples:

Laura is a single mother and full-time caregiver for her elderly father, who has been diagnosed with Parkinson's disease. Every day, Laura is caught in the push-and-pull of work deadlines, her father's medical appointments, her children's needs, and household responsibilities. Her employer expects her to be available outside of regular hours to answer emails and participate in meetings, which leaves her no time to unwind or recharge. She hasn't been able to take a vacation in over two years, and when she does take a break, it's overshadowed by the guilt of leaving her father in someone else's care. In the rare moments Laura does manage to carve out time for herself, she spends more time organizing the logistics of caregiving than actually enjoying her personal time. As a result, Laura feels like she's slowly losing herself in the constant balancing act.

Alex is a healthcare worker who spends long shifts caring for patients in a hospital. Outside of work, he's also the primary caregiver for his mother, who has been recovering from a stroke. On top of his job, he's responsible for managing his mother's rehabilitation appointments, medications, and day-to-day care. Alex tries to take care of his own health by exercising, but he finds himself canceling workout sessions or cutting them short because he's overwhelmed with always caring for others. Despite his best efforts to maintain balance, the constant tug-of-war between work, caregiving, and personal life has started to affect his physical and mental well-being. His work-life balance is nonexistent, leaving him drained and frustrated.

Dean frequently expresses frustration to his wife Megan that they never spend quality time together, as all of her focus is on caring for their son with disabilities, work, and household chores. When they do get time together, Megan is usually too exhausted to do the activities that they used to enjoy as a couple. Even when she tries to get respite, the effort involved in setting it all up and training the staff person ends up being even more tiring.

Jacinta's mother has been diagnosed with cancer and the treatments are not working. Her mother is now palliative and her condition fluctuates from day-to-day. Jacinta has no choice but to go on unpaid leave from work to care for her mother, but she doesn't qualify for financial assistance programs due to restrictive eligibility requirements.

Carla is taking her father to an appointment at 3:00 today at the hospital. They have waited months for the appointment and they are both anxious to see the specialist. She is at work but has arranged to leave early in spite of being under a tight deadline for a project she is working on. She receives a call while she is at work from someone at the hospital saying "We need you to be here at 11:15 am or else we will have to cancel the appointment." Carla looks at the clock and realizes that it is 10:30 am. She doesn't have time to leave work, pick up her father and get to the hospital. The employee cancels the appointment and rebooks it for 3 months later.

Recommendations for Family Caregivers:

- **Clarify Expectations Early**: Caregiving often begins with an unspoken assumption that you'll handle everything, but it's essential to communicate early with healthcare providers, family members, and professionals about the scope of your caregiving role. Set clear boundaries and expectations from the outset to prevent future misunderstandings and stress.

- **Create a Care Plan**: Drafting a caregiving plan with specific roles and responsibilities can help keep things organized and better distribute tasks between caregivers. Include critical details such as appointments, medication schedules, and household chores. A well-organized plan helps ease the mental load of caregiving and ensures everyone knows their responsibilities.
- **Request Regular Check-ins**: Schedule consistent check-ins with healthcare providers or family members to discuss any changes in the care plan and adjust expectations accordingly. Regular updates allows caregivers to express concerns, receive support, and prevent feelings of isolation or overwhelm.
- **Schedule Regular Breaks**: Block off time where other take on caregiving responsibility at regular intervals that you can count on. Consistency makes it easier to plan around and maintain without extra work.
- **Don't Be Afraid to Ask Questions**: It's easy to feel overwhelmed by the amount of information coming your way. Don't hesitate to ask for clarification on any tasks, duties, or schedules that seem unclear. Asking questions ensures you have the support and knowledge needed to care for your loved one.
- **Know Your Rights**: Investigate benefits from work and government programs that can provide assistance for you as a caregiver. Reach out to community agencies and support groups that can help you understand what is available and how you can apply.

Recommendations for Professionals:

- **Establish Clear Roles Early**: From the first meeting, providers should help caregivers clearly define their roles and responsibilities along with that of the care team. This early communication can prevent confusion and unnecessary stress as the caregiving journey progresses and provide caregivers with needed information of who to reach out to when.
- **Set Realistic Expectations**: Professionals should be mindful of what family caregivers can reasonably handle. Avoid placing unreasonable demands on caregivers and offer practical support, such as respite care or guidance on time management, to help them fulfill their responsibilities without sacrificing their well-being.
- **Provide Written Guidelines**: Caregivers often face overwhelming tasks. Providing clear, written instructions for duties like medication administration, therapy regimens, or medical appointments can help caregivers feel more confident and organized.
- **Communicate Regularly**: Professionals should schedule periodic check-ins with caregivers to address any issues or concerns. Open and consistent communication fosters trust and ensures caregivers don't feel like they're navigating the complexities of care alone.
- **Coordinate Care**: Be mindful when scheduling appointments that there are many demands placed on the caregiver (and the patient) and that juggling and attending everything can be a challenge. Last minute changes to appointments might not be feasible for the caregiver to shift things around.
- **Refers for Supports Early**: Connect caregivers with supports and services early in their caregiving journey so that they can establish routines, trust, and relationships with

staff and organizations. This will ensure that when demands increase, they will have ready access without additional demands of looking and applying for help.
- **Think Creatively**: If supports and services have waitlists or service limitations, think creatively about what other supports may exist to help reduce tasks. For example, meal services, lawn care and snow removal, and grocery delivery are all things that can alleviate some of the responsibilities of caregivers allowing them time and energy to perform other tasks.

Recommendations for Organizations:

- **Develop Role-Specific Training**: Offer training programs for caregivers so they are well-prepared for the tasks ahead. Proper training ensures that caregivers have the skills and knowledge to meet the demands of their caregiving roles without feeling overwhelmed.
- **Use Checklists**: Implement comprehensive checklists for caregivers to stay organized and ensure they don't miss any crucial tasks. Checklists can also help reduce the mental burden and improve efficiency.
- **Be Flexible**: Recognize that caregiving roles can evolve over time. Offer flexibility to caregivers in their work hours or caregiving duties, particularly when their loved one's needs change. Being adaptable will prevent burnout and improve their ability to manage both work and caregiving responsibilities.
- **Facilitate Team-Based Care**: Encourage collaboration among multiple caregivers and professionals. Clearly define each person's responsibilities and ensure smooth transitions of care. This reduces the burden on family caregivers and ensures consistent, high-quality care for their loved ones.

- **Have Contingency Staffing**: Caregivers rely on the paid caregivers to show up when they are supposed to. While life happens, contingency plans for trained replacement staff and coverage allows caregivers to depend on the services they need to maintain caregiving and work responsibilities.
- **Become a Caregiver-Friendly Workplace**: Being a caregiver-friendly workplace goes beyond leaves, and flexible work arrangements. Creating an environment of psychological safety where employees can raise their caregiving responsibilities without fear of stigma, biases, or repercussions, and building the mechanisms for leaders to support caregivers, will build stronger teams and enhance recruitment and retention strategies.

Recommendations for Policy Makers:

- **Create Standardized Care Plans**: Policies should encourage providers to create standardized care plans that clearly outline the roles and responsibilities of caregivers, professionals, and patients. This clarity can help reduce confusion and improve coordination of care.
- **Promote Caregiver Education**: Fund programs that provide education and training for caregivers. Proper training ensures caregivers are equipped to manage the demands of their caregiving roles, which helps maintain balance and well-being.
- **Set Legal Guidelines for Caregiving Roles**: Establish clear legal frameworks regarding the rights and responsibilities of caregivers, including job security and protections and financial assistance. This can reduce ambiguity and ensure caregivers are not overloaded with unreasonable demands, offering them legal protections from potential exploitation.

- **Support Family-Centred Care:** Advocate for policies that promote family-centred care, where caregivers are treated as integral members of the care team. Clear communication and agreed-upon roles can make caregiving more manageable and less isolating.
- **Stabilize Workforces**: Caregivers rely on support workers to provide care for their person and respite for them. Stabilization of the workforce through fair wages, regular hours, benefits, and other mechanisms will ensure that they are there when they are needed.

Key Takeaways:

1. **Balance is Key to Preventing Burnout**: A lack of work-life balance can lead to emotional and physical exhaustion for family caregivers.
2. **Set Up Supports Early**: Caregivers should clarify expectations early, create care plans, and communicate regularly with healthcare providers and family members. Professionals should offer clear roles, realistic expectations, and written guidelines to support caregivers.
3. **Employers Can Support Caregivers**: Organizations can enhance benefits and policies that support caregivers and offer flexible work arrangements when possible to reduce caregiver stress.
4. **Governments Can Play a Key Role**: Policymakers should develop guidelines and fund programs and services for standardized care planning, caregiver education, and legal protections to improve caregivers' work-life balance.

Summary:

The struggle to maintain a work-life balance is one of the most significant challenges family caregivers face. Between work, caregiving duties, and personal life, finding time for oneself often seems impossible. The emotional and physical toll of caregiving without sufficient support leads to burnout and exhaustion. It's essential for family caregivers to set boundaries, clarify roles, and create organized care plans. Healthcare professionals and organizations must offer clear guidelines, flexible policies, and regular communication to support caregivers. Policymakers can advocate for standardized care plans, better legal protections, and caregiver education to help prevent caregiver burnout and promote a healthy balance between work and caregiving.

Chapter 10: Excessive Workload, Unclear Expectations and Role Ambiguity

"I thought I knew what caregiving meant. I thought it was just helping someone get through the day. But I was wrong. Caregiving is not just about them. It's about who you become in the process—and who you lose along the way."

When employees are unclear about their roles or what is expected of them, it often leads to confusion, anxiety, and inefficiency. This is also true for caregivers, many of whom struggle with uncertainty about their responsibilities, especially when multiple family members are involved or when the care recipient's needs shift unexpectedly. This lack of clarity can lead to frustration and feelings of inadequacy, compounded by healthcare systems and policies that sometimes create conflicting or vague expectations for family caregivers.

One of the most significant differences between professional and family caregivers is that caregiving isn't just a job — it's their lives. Unlike professionals who can move on to the next client or take a sick day, family caregivers cannot simply clock out. There's no vacation or "closing the door" at the end of the day. They cannot separate themselves from the role, nor do they want to. There are emotional connections that make the experience meaningful, yet also deeply challenging.

While caregiving is often seen as an act of kindness, the reality can be far more complicated. It's an all-consuming responsibility that permeates every aspect of life. Caregivers are invested emotionally and physically, which can make the work deeply meaningful but also exhausting. Over time, the constant demands and shifting responsibilities can erode personal boundaries and even a sense of self. Roles change as relationships evolve — a child may become the caregiver for a parent, or a parent may care for a child with disabilities — and these shifts alter the dynamics and expectations in profound ways. The combination of emotional investment, evolving roles, and relentless pressure can lead to neglect of self, frustration, and burnout.

This overwhelming responsibility can lead to neglect of self, eroding the boundaries between caregiver and who they are as a person. Constant demands, unrealistic expectations, and the pressure to fill gaps in professional services create further frustration, often leading to burnout. The workload, both emotionally and physically draining, can leave caregivers feeling inadequate, overwhelmed, and even lost. With healthcare systems placing unrealistic demands and waiting lists growing longer, the burden often falls squarely on caregivers who have no other choice but to take on more than they can handle.

What makes caregiving so uniquely difficult is not just the demands of the job, it's the lack of recognition, support, and understanding for the critical work family caregivers do. Asking for help and sharing their challenges should be a way to receive support, yet it often results in criticism or blame. This can leave caregivers feeling even more insecure, reinforcing the negative voices that tell them they're failing and fostering their feelings of shame. If caregiving were a professional job, these conditions would be unacceptable. Why, then, is it so common for caregivers to endure such challenges with little support or understanding?

Examples:

Jenna, a caregiver for her elderly mother, found herself in a constant tug-of-war with her family about what her role should be. One family member suggested she should be doing more, while another felt she was doing too much. The lack of communication only deepened her sense of confusion. Jenna didn't know where her responsibility ended or when it was acceptable to ask for help. Was she overstepping by seeking outside support? Should she be doing more for her mother, even though her health was deteriorating rapidly? This lack of clarity created ongoing stress, self-doubt, and an overwhelming sense of inadequacy. She needed guidance, but instead, she found herself caught in an unspoken, emotionally draining cycle.

Carlos is caring for his wife, who has recently been diagnosed with Alzheimer's. As his wife appeared to understand, staff would explain this to her when Carlos wasn't present. While he tries his best to manage her daily needs, he is frequently confronted with medical decisions he is unprepared for. The hospital discharged his wife with instructions that were vague and unclear to him, as they believed his wife understood and remembered the teaching they'd done. The healthcare team assumed he understood the aftercare process, but no one had properly explained the specifics. Carlos found himself making crucial decisions about medication and therapy without adequate information, causing him to second-guess his every move. This left Carlos feeling isolated but also put a strain on his ability to care for his wife with confidence.

Alice's days blurred together as she tried to juggle her mother's medical needs, household chores, and constant doctor's appointments. One morning, the care coordinator handed Alice a stack of paperwork that seemed endless, saying "You'll need to get this all done before the appointment this week," as if that was the easiest thing in the world. Alice barely had time to catch her breath before the next task piled on. With no one else to turn to, she felt the weight of her own exhaustion pressing down harder each day. Alice wasn't just caregiving; she was drowning.

Linda was working and trying to keep up her household while caring for her father. But between his physical needs, and the constant stream of appointments, the house was the last thing on her mind. Plus it had just snowed and she needed to shovel to keep the driveway and steps clear in case her father needed emergency services or they had to get to an appointment. When family members came over and commented on the dust or clutter, Linda's stomach twisted. They didn't understand. It wasn't laziness, it was survival. The pressure to meet everyone's expectations left Linda feeling like she was failing, no matter how hard she worked.

Mark had always been there for his sister who is impacted by chronic mental health issues, but after he started caring for their elderly mother, the demands on his time became overwhelming. When his sister called, asking him to drop everything to come help with an emergency, he felt cornered. "I can't keep doing this!" he thought, but he didn't have the heart to say it out loud. Every time he tried to explain how much he was already managing, he was met with guilt trips or silence. The expectations never stopped, and Mark felt like he was being torn apart in the process.

Emily had been taking care of her husband through multiple surgeries. When the hospital finally decided it was time for him to go home, the discharge planner handed her a list of medical tasks: ostomy care, administering medications, monitoring blood pressure, and said, "You can handle this, right?" Emily felt her heart race. She hadn't been trained for any of this. The hospital had no follow-up plan for her, leaving her to figure it all out on her own while also managing the day-to-day care. She was expected to perform without help, and it was too much.

As soon as Tom's father was discharged from the hospital, the medical team handed him a stack of instructions, leaving him to provide 24/7 care with some assistance from home care services. A week had passed and nobody had shown up from the home care agency. He was on his own. There was no respite care, no backup, no one offering to step in when he was burned out. Tom wasn't just caring for his father; he was keeping a life from falling apart, alone.

"I can't just call in sick, take a vacation, close the door at the end of the day and go home, switch assignments with a colleague, or even move on to the next patient. This is not my job, it is my life."

Recommendations for Family Caregivers:

- **Clarify Expectations**: Right from the start, open a conversation with providers, other family members, and the person you're caring for. It's essential to set clear expectations about your role and responsibilities. Discuss everything from medical care to daily tasks, and ensure everyone is on the same page. This helps prevent misunderstandings and reduces the emotional strain of feeling uncertain about what is expected of you.
- **Write Down Responsibilities**: Consider drafting a caregiving plan or checklist. Having a written document helps clarify your responsibilities and serves as a valuable reference as your caregiving duties evolve. It can include things like medication schedules, doctor's appointments, and specific tasks such as meal preparation or physical

therapy exercises. A written plan will ensure that nothing important gets overlooked.
- **Set Boundaries**: One of the biggest challenges caregivers face is knowing where to draw the line. Establishing and communicating personal boundaries around your caregiving role is crucial. Be clear about what you are willing and able to do and, importantly, where you may need assistance. This not only ensures your own well-being but also creates a framework for others to understand and respect your limits.
- **Request Regular Updates**: Keep an open line of communication with the healthcare team, family members, and any professional caregivers involved in your loved one's care. Request regular updates, especially if there are any changes in your loved one's health or care needs. As circumstances change, the tasks and responsibilities may shift, and staying informed ensures you can adjust accordingly.
- **Set Realistic Goals**: Break down the overwhelming tasks into smaller, manageable goals. Prioritize what's most urgent, and don't hesitate to delegate when possible. Giving yourself realistic expectations can make a huge difference in maintaining your well-being.
- **Advocate for Yourself and Your Loved One**: Speak up about what you can and cannot do and ask for support and services, especially at more stressful times like just after a hospital discharge. Don't hesitate to call agencies to inquire about staffing and alert them to no shows or delays in the start of services and the impact.
- **Have a Contingency Plan**: Emergencies happen. Have a plan in place for when you need immediate help, whether it's a backup caregiver, medical supplies, or emergency contacts. Knowing you're prepared can ease some of the stress.

- **Communicate Openly with Family Members**: Talk about the caregiving duties with everyone involved, especially when things change unexpectedly. Everyone should understand their role and responsibilities, so you're not left with the burden of trying to manage everything alone.
- **Track Tasks and Responsibilities**: Use a calendar or app to track caregiving duties and schedules. It can help you see what's on your plate, prioritize tasks, and reduce the likelihood of missing important tasks.

"Caregiving is supposed to be an act of love, but for many, it's the slow unraveling of their own sense of self."

Recommendations for Professionals:

- **Provide Clear Guidelines**: It's critical for professionals to give caregivers clear, written instructions regarding the care that needs to be provided. This might include responsibilities like medication administration, specialized care instructions or completing application forms. Written guidelines and timelines ensure caregivers have the resources and knowledge to perform their tasks with confidence.
- **Offer Ongoing Support**: Professionals should regularly check in with family caregivers to provide guidance and address any concerns. Caregiving is not a static role, and as care needs evolve, so too must the support provided to caregivers. Offering periodic check-ins and advice can help prevent confusion and keep caregivers feeling supported.
- **Encourage Communication**: Create a collaborative environment where caregivers feel comfortable voicing concerns or asking questions. Caregiving is often filled with uncertainty, and regular communication between

caregivers and professionals can clear up ambiguities and ensure the caregiver feels empowered to make informed decisions.
- **Provide Flexible Care Plans**: Work with caregivers to create flexible care plans that can be adapted to changes in the patient's condition or unexpected caregiving demands. Flexibility is key to easing stress and maintaining a manageable workload.
- **Offer Emergency Resources**: Make sure caregivers are aware of emergency resources, such as urgent care services, home health aides, or after-hours support. This will give them peace of mind knowing they can get help when things become overwhelming.
- **Prepare Caregivers for Emergencies**: Many caregivers don't have medical training, yet they're asked to manage complex situations. Offer training or guidance on how to handle common medical emergencies so they feel more prepared and supported.
- **Collaborate with Family Networks**: Support caregivers by encouraging them to reach out to a broader network of other relatives, friends or care providers, who can step in during times of increased demand or unpredictability. Having a network in place can help share the responsibility and avoid caregiver burnout.
- **Respect Boundaries:** Understand that family caregivers are doing their best. Respect their limits and offer compassion when possible. Know that their situation is difficult, and they need support, not additional stress.

"Caregivers are often expected to shoulder enormous emotional and physical burdens, but when they seek help, they are ignored, belittled, or even punished. A system designed to help is too often a system that harms. There's no EAP

(Employee Assistance Program) for family caregivers, no workplace policies to prevent retaliation from professionals or institutions. In fact, caregivers are frequently left to navigate a web of exclusion and mistreatment, from the person they care for to the organizations that are supposed to offer support."

Recommendations for Organizations:

- **Set Clear Care Plans**: Every patient should have a detailed, written care plan that clearly outlines the expectations for both family caregivers and healthcare providers. This ensures that roles and responsibilities are defined and understood, reducing confusion and improving the quality of care.
- **Offer Caregiver Training**: Caregiver training is critical to ensuring caregivers feel equipped to handle their responsibilities. By offering educational resources and training sessions, organizations can help caregivers build the skills they need to manage their duties effectively and confidently. Caregivers should be included during discharge or other care-related teaching is done to ensure that the patient is properly supported at home.
- **Create Contingency Care Plans**: Develop systems that allow family caregivers to access backup services, like home health aides or emergency respite care. These plans should include flexible scheduling and on-call support to avoid overwhelming caregivers during times of need.
- **Offer Flexible Work Solutions**: For organizations employing caregivers, provide flexible work hours, paid leave, or remote work options to accommodate caregiving responsibilities, especially during emergencies or last-

minute changes. This will help caregivers balance work with caregiving responsibilities without jeopardizing their own well-being.
- **Coordinate with Community Resources**: Establish partnerships with community-based organizations that can provide ongoing and backup support or emergency services. This creates a safety net for caregivers and helps reduce the burden on them.

Recommendations for Policy Makers:

- **Establish National Guidelines**: Fund and support the creation of national or regional guidelines regarding the roles and responsibilities of caregivers. Such guidelines can offer clear expectations and provide a framework for ensuring caregivers are supported and recognized for their contributions.
- **Support Caregiver Education**: Fund initiatives aimed at providing caregivers with the training they need to manage complex tasks. Programs that teach essential caregiving skills and provide guidance on legal rights and available support will help alleviate confusion and improve outcomes for caregivers and care recipients alike. Further, younger caregivers should be supported to continue their education, including post-secondary education, in a way that allows for balance between study, work and caregiving.
- **Create Legal Protections**: Family caregivers should have a clear, legal understanding of their rights and responsibilities. Legal protections that outline caregiver duties, financial benefits and protections, and access to resources are critical to ensuring caregivers are treated fairly and are not left in the dark about their role.
- **Create Emergency Caregiving Policies**: Develop, implement and fund policies and services to provide

backup caregiving options that can step in during emergencies. This could include community-based programs or services that give caregivers reliable, short-term support during times of crisis. This will ensure continuity of care and provides caregivers with a safety net for when caregivers experience burnout or unforeseen events such as an illness that requires they step away temporarily from caregiver duties. This ensures continuity of care even when unexpected events occur.

- **Support Flexible Work for Caregivers**: Create policies that allow caregivers to have flexible work schedules, paid leave, and job protection. This would allow caregivers to balance their caregiving duties without the constant threat of financial or career loss.
- **Implement a National Caregiver Support Strategy:** Advocate for a comprehensive, nationwide support system that provides caregivers with accessible services, including respite care, mental health support, financial assistance, and legal protection. This system would help alleviate the burden on family caregivers.
- **Promote Caregiver Advocacy and Representation:** Ensure that caregivers have a voice in policymaking processes by encouraging caregiver organizations and support groups to advocate for policies that address the needs of those providing family care.
- **Create a "Caregiver Assistance Program (CAP)" for Caregivers:** Just like traditional employees, family caregivers need support. Implementing an CAP tailored to caregivers can provide resources, counselling, and practical support during challenging times.

Key Takeaways:

1. **Unrealistic Expectations Create Burnout:** Family caregivers often face workloads that are physically and emotionally exhausting. The unrealistic demands placed on them can lead to burnout, stress, and a sense of inadequacy. Support and flexibility from both professionals and organizations are essential to mitigating this.
2. **Caregiver Support is Essential:** Without proper support — whether through respite care, flexible work options, or emergency resources — caregivers are left to manage overwhelming responsibilities on their own. Systems and organizations must step up to create solutions that work for caregivers and their loved ones.
3. **Caregivers Deserve Respect and Compassion:** Caregiving is not a 9-to-5 job. It's a full-time role that often comes with physical, emotional, and mental strain. Both professionals and organizations must treat caregivers with empathy, understanding that their needs are just as important as the ones they care for.
4. **Policy Changes Can Ease the Burden:** Government action is necessary to provide comprehensive, long-term support for family caregivers. This includes ensuring they have access to emergency care, financial assistance, and flexible work options to balance caregiving and personal well-being.

Summary:

Family caregiving is one of the most demanding roles a person can take on. Unlike typical work environments where employees can clock out at the end of the day, family caregivers are expected to handle 24/7 responsibilities without sufficient support. The emotional, physical, and mental toll of caregiving is often exacerbated by unrealistic expectations, excessive workloads, and the unpredictable nature of caregiving demands. These challenges leave many caregivers feeling isolated, overwhelmed, and under-appreciated.

However, there is hope. With proper support from professionals, organizations, and policymakers, the strain of caregiving can be alleviated. Caregivers need flexible care plans, access to emergency resources, and a more empathetic understanding from both the healthcare system and their communities. Policies that support caregivers, such as emergency respite care, flexible work hours, and caregiver leave, are crucial in helping them manage their responsibilities without sacrificing their own health and well-being.

By recognizing the immense value of family caregivers and providing them with the support they deserve, we can begin to build a system that prioritizes both those receiving care and those giving it.

Chapter 11: Gossip and Negative Social Dynamics

"I already feel like a failure. That I don't know enough, am not strong enough, am not patient enough, kind enough. I go to bed every night thinking of all the ways I could have been better. To overhear comments by staff, or worse, see it in writing somewhere, is devastating. It reinforces all of the bad things I say to myself. I want to scream that I am always, every single minute, just trying to do the best I can in the situation that I am in."

Gossip and negative social dynamics can have a profound impact on caregivers. A workplace or family environment filled with gossip, backstabbing, or judgment can create a toxic atmosphere that erodes trust and fosters insecurity. This can be even more damaging when the gossip is overheard by family caregivers, leaving them feeling alienated, judged, or inadequate. Family members or even professionals may inadvertently spread misinformation, criticize caregiving methods, or engage in negative talk that increases the caregiver's stress and self-doubt. Whether it's a dismissive comment from a staff member or an unhelpful critique from a relative, these interactions can leave caregivers feeling unsupported and overwhelmed. As a result, caregivers may feel more isolated, question their ability to care for their loved one, and struggle with increased emotional strain.

Examples:

John, a son taking care of his elderly father, constantly feels undermined by his siblings. One sibling criticizes his father's medical care, saying, "You're doing it all wrong," without offering any suggestions or support. They gossip about his "lack of patience" and criticize him for not "doing enough," even though they have no idea what he goes through daily. The constant criticism, without constructive help, leaves John feeling isolated and inadequate, questioning his decisions, and struggling to keep up with the demands of caregiving.

In a visit from a social worker, Tanya, a caregiver for her disabled brother, overhears comments made by the social worker about her "lack of involvement" in certain decisions and yet is "demanding" when she advocates for her brother. These offhand remarks make Tanya feel judged, even though she is actively trying to balance caregiving with her own personal and professional life, leading to feelings of inadequacy, increasing her stress. It also breeds a sense of mistrust and uncertainty that affects her ability to engage fully with the healthcare team.

In a local caregiver support group, professionals and peers gossip about other caregivers in the group. They share unverified stories about how certain caregivers are "too emotional" or "not strong enough," making others in the group feel uncomfortable and reluctant to share their own struggles. This toxic environment discourages open discussion and contributes to a lack of trust and support among caregivers.

Recommendations for Family Caregivers:

- **Trust Your Instincts**: If you find yourself questioning your decisions because of negative comments or gossip, remember that you are doing your best in a challenging

situation. Trust in your abilities as a caregiver and rely on your knowledge of your loved one's needs.
- **Set Boundaries with Family and Professionals**: If you experience negative comments from family or professionals, calmly set boundaries by addressing the issue directly. You might say, "I understand you have concerns, but I'm doing my best. If you have suggestions or want to help, I'm open to discussing them in a constructive way."
- **Seek Out Supportive Communities**: Find and engage in positive, supportive caregiving communities — whether in person or online. Avoid groups or spaces where gossip and negativity thrive. Surround yourself with individuals who uplift you and who share similar caregiving challenges.
- **Focus on Self-Care and Reflection**: When you feel overwhelmed by negative feedback or criticism, take time for self-care. Practice mindfulness, journaling, or simply stepping away from the situation to regain perspective. Reflect on your efforts and remind yourself of the positive impact you're making in your loved one's life.
- **Document Harmful Interactions**: If you feel that gossip or negative interactions are affecting your caregiving environment, consider documenting these occurrences. Keeping a record will help you better understand patterns and take action if necessary, whether that's addressing the issue directly or seeking outside support.

"It all gets downloaded onto me. There's things I need to know and things I don't. Telling me might lighten them but then....I am left to carry it....on tup of my own stuff. Boundaries don't solve this. Not when it affects your person, and therefore you. It gets so hard to breathe through it all. The weight

crushes me. Yet I have to carry on for my person. Who do I get to unload to? Who takes care of me?"

Recommendations for Professionals:

- **Model Positive Social Dynamics**: Healthcare professionals should create an environment that fosters respect and collaboration. They should lead by example by avoiding gossip and instead creating spaces for caregivers to openly express concerns and share experiences.
- **Be Mindful of Language and Judgments**: Professionals should be aware of the language they use when interacting with caregivers and avoid making offhand remarks that could be perceived as judgmental. If offering feedback or advice, it should be done constructively and with empathy.
- **Establish Confidentiality and Trust**: Professionals must maintain confidentiality and ensure that caregivers feel safe in expressing their needs without fear of gossip or judgment. They should actively discourage negative talk and create a supportive atmosphere where caregivers can be honest and vulnerable.
- **Provide Clear, Positive Communication**: Instead of engaging in negative discussions or assumptions, healthcare professionals should provide caregivers with clear, actionable guidance. When addressing any concerns, they should focus on solutions rather than criticisms.

Recommendations for Organizations:

- **Create a Culture of Respect and Transparency**: Organizations should actively promote a culture of respect and transparency among staff and caregivers. This includes

training staff on the importance of non-judgmental language.
- **Offer Support Networks for Caregivers**: Organizations should establish caregiver support groups where individuals can share experiences in a safe, confidential, and supportive environment. These groups should be free from gossip and should focus on mutual support and constructive feedback.
- **Implement Anti-Gossip Policies**: Implement clear policies that outline the expectation for respectful communication and prohibit gossip in caregiving environments. Staff should be held accountable for creating a supportive environment that enhances caregiver well-being.
- **Encourage Professional Development**: Provide training for professionals on how to handle sensitive conversations with caregivers, emphasizing empathy, compassion, and the need to avoid negative language or criticism.
- **Documentation Standards**: Documentation standards and policies should direct professionals to state objective observations and assessments and avoid language that makes judgements about caregivers.

Recommendations for Policy Makers:

- **Advocate for Caregiver Protections**: Policy makers should advocate for laws and regulations that protect caregivers from workplace gossip, discrimination, and negative social dynamics. This may include enforcing anti-retaliation policies and ensuring that caregivers have a safe space to voice concerns.
- **Provide Funding for Caregiver Support Programs**: Governments should allocate funding to support caregiver networks and resources that promote positive interactions and minimize the harmful effects of gossip and negative social dynamics.

- **Establish National Standards for Caregiver Support**: Create national standards for caregiver support that prioritize emotional well-being and ensure caregivers are provided with the resources they need to thrive in their roles without facing undue criticism or judgment.
- **Encourage Anti-Stigma Campaigns**: Government-led campaigns to reduce the stigma associated with caregiving can help break down harmful stereotypes and create a more supportive culture for both caregivers and professionals.

Key Takeaways:

1. **Gossip Has a Negative Impact on Caregivers:** Gossip in caregiving environments, whether at work or within the family, can lead to emotional harm for caregivers. Hearing critical comments, whether direct or indirect, erodes trust and amplifies feelings of inadequacy, causing increased stress. Caregivers often internalize negative comments, leading them to feel isolated and uncertain about their abilities. This emotional strain can make it harder for them to perform effectively and care for their loved ones.
4. **Constructive Support is Key:** Negative feedback should be constructive and offer support, not judgment. Caregivers need a network of people who offer encouragement, not criticism, to maintain their mental health and well-being.
5. **Setting Boundaries and Seeking Positive Environments:** Caregivers can protect themselves by setting clear boundaries with family and professionals who offer negative commentary. Engaging in supportive communities and focusing on self-care is essential for mental resilience.
6. **Professional Responsibility:** Healthcare professionals are urged to create a culture of respect by modelling positive social dynamics and avoiding harmful gossip. Clear, empathetic communication is vital for building trust with caregivers.

Documentation should include objective observations and assessments rather than judgements of caregivers.
7. **Organizational and Policy-Level Change:** Organizations and policy makers should work to create environments free from gossip, offer formal support networks, and provide proper training to minimize the harmful effects of negative social dynamics on caregivers.

Summary:

Gossip and negative social dynamics can have a profound negative impact on caregivers. In environments where negative comments, judgements, or gossip are prevalent, whether within the family, among professionals, or within caregiving communities, caregivers often feel unsupported and emotionally drained. These toxic dynamics breed mistrust and self-doubt, further increasing stress and isolation for those already under significant pressure. Fostering positive, respectful environments where caregivers are offered constructive feedback, emotional support, and trust will also foster collaborative relationships. Caregivers must protect their well-being by taking actions such as setting boundaries, seeking out supportive communities, and engaging in self-care. Professionals and organizations are encouraged to create cultures of respect and to provide clear, actionable communication. Policy makers need to establish regulations and funding to support caregivers, ensuring they are shielded from harmful dynamics and provided with the resources to thrive.

Chapter 12: Inconsistent Workflows, Processes and Staffing

"I feel like I'm constantly running in circles. Each new doctor or professional tells me something different. The forms, the appointments, the new procedures, everything seems to be at odds with each other or there is so much duplication that I fill out the same information several times for the same organization. I've never felt so overwhelmed, yet no one can explain why it's so disorganized. I just want things to work smoothly for once."

Inconsistent workflows and processes can be a major source of frustration for family caregivers. This disorganization can manifest in multiple ways, such as duplicate paperwork, variations in caregiving practices, lack of information transfer between providers, and confusion over procedures. When caregivers are required to repeat the same information to multiple professionals or are given conflicting advice, it leads to feelings of being unheard and that their input is insignificant. The lack of structure in caregiving environments makes it harder for caregivers to stay organized, follow through with care plans, and deliver the best possible care to their loved one. These inefficiencies not only increase stress but also create delays that affect the quality and timeliness of care.

Examples:

Emily is filling out forms for a home health agency that already has much of her mother's information. Despite this, she's asked to repeat the same details on different forms, which only adds to her administrative burden and frustration. Each time she submits information, it feels like it falls into a void, as nothing seems to be shared among healthcare providers.

When different healthcare workers visit Sally's mother, each professional follows a slightly different approach to managing care. One nurse has specific instructions for administering medications, while another has a different process, leaving Sally confused and worried that she's not doing it right. This lack of consistency makes it difficult for her to feel confident in the care being provided.

Kerry wasn't told that the regular care provider from the agency wasn't available to come and assist her mother. The staff person that arrives is unfamiliar with her mother, her needs and individual preferences. Kerry's mother starts to become upset that the care provider is not doing things the way she prefers. Kerry ends up doing the care herself while "training" the new care provider. This means that she is unable to complete the other tasks that she had planned to do which will have her getting even further behind in everything.

Jackie is given the wrong forms to fill out when she attempts to request additional services for her mother. This causes delays in getting the necessary help, and once she fills out the correct forms, the process is delayed even further with phone interviews and more paperwork. The time wasted on paperwork feels like a drain on her energy and attention, which could be better spent caring for her mother.

The constant turnover in staff at the group home has Simon, who is a non-verbal autistic gentleman, anxious and stressed and grieving the loss of the staff he likes. He communicates with his mother via communication tools. The anxiety and stress means he is reaching out to his mother multiple times a day. She is too far away to go visit him as regularly as she would like and is strained, distressed and feeling guilty that she can't bring him home during rough patches like this. Lately the staff turnover has been constant and now aggressive behaviours are becoming more frequent adding to the turnover in staff who are uncomfortable with managing the anxiety to mitigate and prevent the aggressive behaviours and manage the resulting outburst. Simon's mother feels helpless.

Recommendations for Family Caregivers:

- **Stay Organized**: Caregivers should create a consistent routine to track appointments, medications, tasks, and follow-up needs. Digital tools, such as apps or calendars, can help streamline this process and reduce confusion.
- **Advocate for Structured Plans**: Speak up and request structured care plans and clear schedules from care providers. Having a consistent plan in place can reduce unpredictability and minimize the chances of conflicting or incomplete care instructions.
- **Advocate for Standardized Forms**: Advocate for standardization in paperwork and centralized intake processes where one form can be used for multiple organizations. Further, advocate for right information/right time in accordance with privacy legislation where only the required information can be gathered to prevent oversharing on preliminary intake forms. Whenever possible, present providers with copies of forms that you

have already completed for other organizations. Sometimes they will accept them without having their own forms completed and then only request any varying information. When you are faced with multiple forms from the same provider with duplicate information requested, highlight this to the provider and only complete the information once on the provider-preferred form.

- **Seek Continuity of Care**: Request consistency in the care providers or team who come into your home or manage your loved one's care, to avoid disruption in care and ensure stability. Further, advocate for a plan of action when this continuity can't be maintained (life happens). Consistency in care providers can reduce variations in treatment and ensure a more predictable caregiving experience.
- **Track Changes**: Keep a log of any changes in care, health status, or treatment. Tracking variations can help you identify patterns and bring up any concerns with healthcare professionals in a more organized manner.
- **Create Your Own Routines**: While caregiving can be unpredictable, developing daily routines can help caregivers manage the chaos. These routines can include regular meal times, medication schedules, and caregiving tasks to ensure that nothing is missed. Keep a detailed record of your loved one's care routines and needs, which can be shared with any new care providers or healthcare professionals to maintain continuity.
- **Track Progress**: Monitor medications, treatments, and progress in a notebook or digital format. This practice can help you stay on top of caregiving tasks and serve as a quick reference when communicating with healthcare providers.
- **Communicate with Healthcare Providers**: If you notice inconsistencies in processes or care, don't hesitate to

communicate your concerns to healthcare providers. Setting up a more structured care plan can ease the burden of uncertainty.
- **Utilize Technology**: Request electronic and fillable forms that you can complete and store on your computer and update as needed. This will reduce the amount of duplication. Advocate for technology use in organizations for appointments to reduce numbers of trips for multiple appointments. Request that appointments be made in a more manageable way using these systems. Advocate for portals that caregivers can access to facilitate care management and coordination. Advocate for consents that can be signed securely electronically to prevent mailing, printing, scanning, faxing and other actions that can delay completion of tasks and increase expenses and time when you don't have these items at home.
- **Prepare for Changes**: Understand that turnover can be inevitable, so keep detailed records of care routines to help new care providers step in smoothly.
- **Stay Involved in Transitions**: During transitions, be proactive in making sure that any new care providers are fully informed about your loved one's needs.
- **Encourage Team Collaboration**: If you're working with a team of care providers, encourage them to communicate regularly and share information to ensure smooth transitions between shifts. Care conferences involving multiple providers and professionals in and across organizations may be beneficial at times where there is added complexity or transitions.

Recommendations for Professionals:

- **Standardize Processes**: Healthcare professionals should standardize processes for communication, patient

management, and care coordination to make workflows clear and manageable for caregivers.
- **Provide Clear Instructions**: Always provide family caregivers with clear, written guidelines on caregiving processes, especially when they involve multiple steps (e.g., administering medications, managing treatments). Detailed instructions ensure caregivers understand the proper methods and responsibilities.
- **Streamline Transitions**: When transitioning care from one professional to another or from one phase of care to another, ensure that there's a smooth handoff with well-documented processes. All relevant information should be well-documented to prevent any gaps in care or confusion for caregivers.
- **Use Technology to Stay Organized**: Adopt and utilize electronic health records and applications with their functionality to streamline care coordination. This can ensure that caregivers and healthcare teams have access to the same up-to-date information.
- **Standardize Care Processes**: Adopt standardized care processes across healthcare teams to ensure consistency in care instructions and execution. This consistency will help family caregivers manage their responsibilities more easily.
- **Coordinate Care Across Teams**: Encourage better coordination between professionals involved in a patient's care, ensuring everyone follows the same workflows. This reduces miscommunication and helps caregivers manage multiple providers more effectively.
- **Provide Resources for Better Organization**: Healthcare providers can offer family caregivers resources such as apps or scheduling tools to help with organizing tasks, making the caregiving process smoother and less stressful.

- **Be Transparent About Transitions**: When changes occur, communicate clearly with caregivers and provide the necessary support to help them adjust.
- **Ensure Smooth Transitions**: Implement systems that allow for easy transitions between healthcare professionals or shifts, such as care logs or briefings that new staff can easily review. Ensure that systems also include caregivers.
- **Incorporate Family Caregiver Input**: Ensure that caregivers' insights are included in any staff handover or care transition process to avoid miscommunication or confusion.
- **Build Strong Relationships**: Build long-term relationships with caregivers to foster trust, continuity, and collaboration.

Recommendations for Organizations:

- **Develop Workflow Systems**: Organizations should invest in or develop electronic health systems that support consistent workflows, reducing errors and improving efficiency across multiple caregivers and healthcare professionals.
- **Create Care Pathways**: Establish standardized care pathways for common conditions or treatments. This gives family caregivers clear expectations for care at each stage of treatment, helping them stay organized and informed.
- **Use Automation Tools**: Implement automation tools such as appointment and medication reminders. These tools can help caregivers stay on top of essential tasks and reduce cognitive load.
- **Implement Collaborative Care Models**: Encourage collaborative models where all professionals involved in care follow a unified approach with shared goals, reducing fragmentation in the care. Ensure caregivers are valued care

partners. A collaborative team environment ensures caregivers don't feel alone in managing care.
- **Develop Integrated Systems**: Create integrated communication systems for healthcare teams and caregivers to minimize miscommunication. Clear channels of information flow are essential for reducing workflow breakdowns and ensuring continuity of care.
- **Use Technology to Streamline Care**: Adopt technology solutions like shared digital care plans or apps that help caregivers better coordinate with healthcare providers. These tools make information-sharing more efficient and reduce administrative tasks.
- **Create Continuity Across Shifts**: For settings where professional caregivers rotate in and out, ensure smooth transitions by providing clear handovers of patient information. This ensures consistency in care and minimizes disruption for both caregivers and their loved ones.
- **Co-Design and Co-Produce Workflows with Patients and Caregivers**: Patients and caregivers should be equal partners not just in co-design but in co-production of workflows and system/organizational changes. This ensures that changes work and are implemented in a way that works for everyone.
- **Create and Invest In Retention Strategies**: Implement retention strategies, such as offering professional development, competitive salaries, flexible schedules, continuing education, job satisfaction initiatives, and other benefits to reduce staff turnover and provide consistency for caregivers.
- **Maintain Consistent Care Teams**: Build teams of care providers who work together collaboratively, allowing them to develop rapport with both the patient and the family.

- **Ensure Clear Handover Processes**: Develop clear handover processes that ensure all information is passed smoothly from one healthcare or social services provider to the next.
- **Develop and Provide Mentorship Programs**: Develop and support mentorship programs where experienced staff can guide new staff members, ensuring continuity in practices, smoother transitions and greater continuity in care.
- **Create Flexible Work Schedules**: Provide flexible work hours or shifts to reduce caregiver burnout and increase job satisfaction, ultimately reducing turnover.

Recommendations for Policy Makers:

- **Support Electronic Health Records**: Policy makers should promote and fund policies that encourage the adoption of interoperable electronic health records. This will streamline care coordination and reduce the fragmentation of information, ensuring caregivers and professionals have access to the same up-to-date data.
- **Standardize Care Protocols**: Advocate for and fund the development and adoption of national or regional care protocols for various diseases and conditions, ensuring that caregivers and healthcare providers are aligned in their approach.
- **Encourage Cross-Disciplinary Collaboration**: Create, implement and promote policies that foster collaboration across healthcare disciplines (e.g., physicians, nurses, therapists, and family caregivers) to ensure smooth transitions and consistent care delivery.
- **Provide Funding for Training**: Invest in programs that train caregivers, care providers, and professionals on a variety of topics such as: how to use digital tools and

systems to enhance communication and streamline workflows and reduce the administrative burden on professionals and caregivers.
- **Promote Technology Use**: Advocate for policies that encourage the use of digital platforms in caregiving, allowing caregivers and healthcare providers to access care information quickly and efficiently, improving care coordination.
- **Standardize Best Practices**: Promote the adoption of standardized best practices to support caregivers at the national level. These practices can help ensure more uniform and predictable workflows across healthcare settings, reducing confusion for caregivers.
- **Encourage Cross-Agency Coordination**: Implement policies that promote cooperation between healthcare providers, insurance agencies, and caregivers, ensuring no gaps or breakdowns in the caregiving process. This cooperation ensures that information is transferred more easily between care team members directly instead of relying on the caregiver to take on this task.
- **Incentivize Long-Term Caregivers**: Create policies that incentivize long-term caregivers, both formal and informal, through tax relief, support benefits, or other financial incentives.
- **Enact Workforce Stability Policies**: Advocate for policies that promote workforce stability within caregiving fields, such as healthcare worker retention bonuses, improved benefits, and opportunities for advancement
- **Support Caregiver Employment**: Create policies that encourage the hiring and retention of professional caregivers in the home care and healthcare sectors, ensuring continuity of care so that family caregivers can continue to work, confident that their person will be cared for while they are gone. Invest in Caregiver-Friendly

Workplace initiatives so that organizations can support their employees who are also family caregivers.
- **Promote Paid Family Leave**: Support policies that provide paid caregiver leaves, health benefits, flexible work policies, and other supportive mechanisms, so caregivers do not have to choose between or leave their work or caregiver roles due to financial strain, ensuring continuity for the person they care for.
- **Implement Strategies that Support Care Provider Recruitment and Retention**: Current funding strategies like the use of funding envelopes to bid on service provision can contribute to an unstable workforce as worker must move around following the contracts which results in restricted pay increase opportunities, a lack of benefits, and a lack of job security. Strategies that maintain wages, hours, benefits and job security will allow for increased consistency in care providers for patients and caregivers, improving quality of care and reducing costs of recruitment, training and other employment costs which are then transferred to the system.

Key Takeaways:

1. **Consistency Benefits Everyone:** Inconsistent workflows and processes can significantly increase the administrative burden on caregivers, making their already demanding roles even more challenging. When workflows are fragmented or not standardized, caregivers may struggle to stay organized, resulting in delays in care and an increase in stress and confusion. Paid care providers that are not trained to work with specific clients and unfamiliar with individual needs and care requirements may add to the caregiver burden if the caregiver must train them. Organizations and the systems they work in benefit with recruitment and retention strategies that decrease

the financial costs and strain caused by constant staffing turnover.
2. **Collaboration and Shared Information Reduces Strain:** The lack of communication between healthcare providers, both within the same organization and across different organizations, often results in caregivers repeating the same information and feeling unheard. Streamlining workflows, providing clear instructions, and improving coordination among healthcare teams are essential steps in easing the caregiving experience and improving care quality.

Summary:

Inconsistent workflows and processes present a significant challenge for family caregivers, leading to stress, confusion, and delays in care. When caregivers face fragmented communication, differing care approaches, and repeated tasks, it not only impacts their well-being but also the quality of care they provide. Standardizing workflows, improving communication, and offering clear, consistent care plans can alleviate much of the burden that caregivers experience. Both professionals and organizations need to adopt structured, streamlined approaches that minimize miscommunication and provide caregivers with the tools they need to stay organized. Recruitment and retention strategies for care providers and professionals will strengthen the health and social services systems and reduce the overall costs. Policymakers also play a crucial role in supporting technological solutions and standardized care practices that improve care coordination and reduce administrative burdens.

Chapter 13: Lack of Career Development Opportunities and Limited Training and Education

"In a toxic workplace, employees are told to 'speak up' about their needs and take care of themselves. But for family caregivers, 'speaking up' can feel like an act of betrayal. 'Taking care of yourself' may seem impossible when you feel responsible for someone else's well-being. And unlike workers who can 'leave,' caregivers often can't walk away without devastating consequences."

Employees in toxic environments often feel stuck with no clear path for growth or advancement. Many caregivers put their personal career development on hold to focus on caregiving, leading to feelings of stagnation or lost opportunities. Ongoing caregiving duties for working caregivers can lead to the neglect of personal career aspirations due to the time and energy demands, making caregivers feel stuck or unable to pursue personal growth or career advancement. Training for caregivers within their caregiving role can be limited or hidden behind barriers such as timing or modality of offerings. This can all contribute to financial strains along with feelings of loss of self and self-worth, and being trapped.

Examples:

Maria is a caregiver for her aging parents and has teenagers at home. She occasionally has to leave work due to appointments or when one of them is ill and needs help. She faces stigma and biases in the workplace due to her caregiving role and absences from work due to caregiving responsibilities. This is making it difficult for her to work on high profile projects as she gets passed over for someone else. As such, she is also not being considered for promotions, training, and skill development opportunities. At her 1:1 with her manager, she requests to receive feedback on how to improve and advance in her career, but her manager is vague and only guides her to opportunities for work that he thinks won't take her away from caregiving duties (as traveling for work or transfers to other locales would).

Sophia has had to put her career on hold with an unpaid leave to provide care to her mother who has been diagnosed with cancer, causing her to fall behind in professional development, career advancement and promotions. She feels that she's missed opportunities for growth due to her caregiving role.

Tim's caregiving schedule is so unpredictable that he can't attend professional development courses or networking events, which all seem to fall outside of working hours, stalling his professional growth. When he does find ones to attend, they are often out-of-town and travelling requires a lot of time and energy lining up respite or other help, if it is available and not too costly.

Ruth is fortunate to have a job that allows her to work-from-home, making it easier for her to juggle her career and caregiving duties. Even with using technology for connecting with her colleagues,

Ruth feels isolated from her professional community because she's been away from the office for so long and can't participate in the office socialization.

Alex had to give up his career aspirations because his workplace doesn't offer flexible work arrangements or family caregiver leave. This has resulted in his not applying for promotions or other positions that will impede his ability to focus on caregiving and juggle all of the demands. Unfortunately he finds it too challenging to attend professional development seminars, networking events, or even job interviews because he cannot find respite care or work around the limited schedules of medical appointments.

Gina receives emails for information sessions on a variety of topics such as financial planning for parents of people with disabilities, Henson Trusts, future housing options, completing applications for new government programs and more. These sessions would really help her better manage her caregiving duties. She would love to attend as she finds it challenging to research all of this on her own and on top of all the other demands, it is overwhelming. Unfortunately, the sessions are only offered in person and at times when she is at her work. She already uses up her sick days, vacation and any personal time with her caregiving responsibilities (she is lucky to have a job where she has these benefits) and therefore is unable to attend.

Recommendations for Family Caregivers:

- **Request Education**: Ask providers for training in specialized caregiving skills, such as medication management, wound care, or handling complex medical equipment.
- **Take Online Courses**: Look for online resources, courses, or webinars that teach caregiving skills specific to the needs of your loved one.

- **Learn From Peers**: Join caregiver networks or support groups where you can learn tips and strategies from others who have been through similar experiences.
- **Advocate for Yourself**: Use check-ins with your managers to outline your career goals and develop a plan for realizing them. Identify opportunities that are available to advance your career. Strengthen your supports and services for caregiving so that assistance is more readily available when networking, education and other opportunities arise.

Recommendations for Professionals:

- **Offer Caregiver Training**: Provide formal training programs for caregivers to equip them with the necessary skills for effective caregiving. Offer training and information sessions at a variety of times and through a variety of modalities e.g. in-person, on-line, recorded webinars, instructional booklets, information packages and more.
- **Include Caregivers in Educational Sessions**: Encourage caregivers to attend medical or therapy appointments with the patient to ensure they are part of the education process.
- **Provide Accessible Resources**: Offer training materials or workshops that caregivers can access at their convenience to improve their skills. Accessibility includes offering remote trainings or if they must be onsite then providing respite so that caregivers can attend.

Recommendations for Organizations:

- **Develop Comprehensive Caregiver Education Programs**: Implement educational programs that address common caregiving challenges and provide clear solutions.

- **Provide Ongoing Training**: Ensure that caregivers receive ongoing training opportunities, so they feel continually supported and up-to-date on care practices.
- **Offer Accessible Learning Materials**: Make educational resources, such as pamphlets, videos, or online courses, easily available to caregivers.
- **Offer Opportunities to Caregivers Equally**: Employers can create mechanisms for monitoring for networking and continuing education opportunities for employees where there is lots of notice. This will provide caregivers with time to make appropriate arrangements for respite or other supports and services so that they can attend. Having discussions with employees about their career aspirations and creating development plans will open the conversation to what is possible and minimize assumptions about what is and isn't.
- **Provide Flexible Education Funds**: Employers can facilitate participation in educational and training opportunities by offering education funds, allowing employees to choose options that are more accessible to all of their needs.

Recommendations for Policy Makers:

- **Invest in Caregiver Education**: Fund programs that provide free or low-cost training for caregivers, making them better equipped to manage complex care needs. Standardized programs will also provide professional recognition of the education and what is included. Organizations should be funded to have education departments that can support the creation of materials for educating caregivers. These materials should be easily customizable by staff for the uniqueness of each patient and caregiver.

- **Create Public Awareness Campaigns**: Promote the importance of caregiving education, encouraging families to pursue training when they take on caregiving roles.
- **Train the Trainers**: Ensure that education of professionals includes caregiver education methodologies and practices. These courses should include how to assess current knowledge of caregivers and the development of individual education plans.
- **Enhance Workplace Protections for Caregivers**: Introduce legislation that supports caregivers, when they need to take leaves from work or can't attend activities outside of working hours related to caregiving responsibilities.

Key Takeaways:

1. **Stagnation Due to Caregiving**: Caregivers often experience career stagnation due to the time and energy caregiving demands, which can prevent them from participating in career advancement opportunities, training, and networking events.
2. **Lack of Workplace Support**: Many workplaces do not provide the necessary flexibility or support for caregivers to manage both their work and caregiving responsibilities, hindering career development.
3. **Need for Training and Education**: There is a lack of accessible training and educational resources for caregivers, which impacts their ability to manage complex care needs and develop skills that would help them professionally.
4. **Barriers to Professional Growth**: Caregivers face barriers like unpredictable schedules, lack of leave options, and limited access to relevant professional development courses or events. This can lead to missed career opportunities.

Summary:

Caregivers often find themselves in tough spots, juggling demanding caregiving roles while trying to keep their careers on track. The lack of career development opportunities, training, and flexible work options leads many caregivers to feel stuck in their current positions, missing out on promotions, skill-building opportunities, and even job satisfaction. Real-life examples, like Maria and Tim, show how difficult it is to keep up with career goals when caregiving takes priority, and how the workplace sometimes doesn't offer enough understanding or flexibility to make it work.

Ultimately a shift in how we think about caregiving and professional growth, job security and a caregivers career aspirations, is needed. While we can encourage caregivers to advocate for themselves, ask for the training they need, and seek support where they can, organizations can offer equal opportunities, create flexible training programs, and open up real conversations about career advancement. With the large number of employed caregivers, there's a strong push and desperate need to improve protections and funding for caregiver education, so they don't have to sacrifice their professional aspirations and can feel confident in their caregiving roles. In the end, it's about creating a more supportive, understanding environment where caregivers can thrive, both at home and at work. Everyone has a role to play in helping them find that balance.

Chapter 14: Fear of Retaliation or Repercussions

"The fear of speaking up is not an abstract idea for family caregivers; it is an ever-present reality. And it's not just about raising concerns about mistreatment; it's about survival. For many caregivers, confronting the toxic systems they interact with means risking everything: losing financial support, facing retaliation from professionals, or being told they're too 'emotional' to make informed decisions. It's not just about the burden of care; it's about carrying the weight of an entire system that was never built to support caregivers. It's a dilemma with no easy answer: speak up and risk losing everything, or stay silent and lose yourself."

A culture of fear surrounds many family caregivers, leaving them hesitant to speak up or advocate for their needs, due to the fear of retaliation or negative repercussions. This fear can manifest in various ways: caregivers may be afraid to raise concerns about their loved one's care, voice dissatisfaction with the services being provided, or ask for respite time. Whether it's the fear of being labeled as a "complainer," or facing actual consequences like losing support, services, or access to critical resources, this fear can create a sense of isolation and emotional distress. Caregivers often find themselves caught in a dilemma: should they voice their concerns and risk their caregiving role, or remain silent and endure the negative impacts on their well-being?

Examples:

James had been the primary caregiver for his wife for years. He was exhausted, but every time he thought about asking for respite, a voice in his head stopped him: "You can't leave her. You're the only one she has. She and the family will never forgive you." When he finally worked up the courage to ask his family for help, they told him he should be stronger. James felt selfish. So, he kept pushing through, burning out quietly, all while the need for rest was pressing on him like a weight.

Sarah is the family caregiver for her father who is in a care home. She has had many concerns about his care over the years and the staff and management now see her as a complainer and difficult family member. They have even taken steps to try and limit who she can speak with on the team and when she can visit her father. She worries that if she brings anything else up that she will be barred from the care home. She knows other families that it has happened to and ever since she heard their stories she fears for her father and herself. She decides it is better to be able to keep visiting him and monitor his condition than speak up about her concerns.

Every evening, Robert would help his mother with dinner, bathe her, and sit with her until she fell asleep. But after weeks of this routine, he was running on empty. One night, when his sister offered to take over for a few hours, Robert didn't say yes - he knew that his sister wasn't reliable and might not show up or do the needed tasks. This had caused arguments in the past and resulted in his sister not speaking to him for months after calling him ungrateful. This also meant his sister stopped seeing their mother. So, he kept doing everything himself, silently resenting the mounting pressure.

Lisa had noticed inconsistencies in the care her aunt was receiving from the home care worker. Medications were being administered late, and her aunt seemed more confused than usual. But when Lisa reported her concerns with the agency, she was told that there were no other workers available. No other options or solutions such as staff training were brought up. They asked Lisa if she wanted to file a formal complaint. Lisa hesitated and then declined. What if the staff turned against her? What if they made things harder for her aunt? So, Lisa kept quiet, questioning if she was imagining the mistakes and feeling trapped by her own fear.

Tom had been struggling with his aging mother's care for months. He was becoming overwhelmed by any extra tasks given to him. When he finally reached out to a social worker, he hoped for some guidance. But when she made him feel as though he wasn't doing enough, citing the example that he still had not completed some forms she had given him, and hinted at his inability to manage, Tom froze. The social worker then asked if he wanted to put his mother in a long term care facility. He didn't want to seem incapable, but he needed more help, not to put his mother in a home. He kept his frustrations to himself, afraid the social worker would take away the current supports he desperately needed.

Tammy's adult son has developmental disabilities and can be physically aggressive. Tammy made the difficult choice to have her son go into a group home when he became too big and strong for her to manage on her own. The group home staff and management listen to what she says about her son and his needs but then none of it is documented and included in the care plan. The group home makes demands on things they want done instead and when she cites the information that she has given them previously as rationale for a different approach, they proceed as they wish, causing distress for Tammy's son when it backfires. Any time she speaks up or declines to do what they want when she knows it is incorrect, there is hostility. Tammy gets a call one day from a Public Guardian and Trustee Office investigator as someone has made a complaint that she is not upholding her duties as legal guardian and taking proper care of her son.

"Caregiving is a role that can quickly become all-consuming. But when a caregiver seeks outside help from healthcare providers, and organizations, what they often find is not compassion, but exclusion, frustration, and sometimes outright hostility. For many caregivers, speaking up about their experiences, whether it's raising concerns about their loved one's treatment, asking for better care plans, or requesting time off from an employer for their own well-being, is viewed as complaints and therefore can result in retaliation. This could mean losing access to critical services, being labeled as difficult or demanding, or, in some cases, losing their role as the primary caregiver altogether."

Recommendations for Family Caregivers:

- **Know Your Rights:** Understand your rights as a caregiver and advocate. Familiarize yourself with laws and policies in your area that protect caregivers from retaliation or discrimination. Knowledge can empower you to take action if necessary.
- **Document Everything:** Keep records of any concerns or incidents, particularly if you feel there is a risk of retaliation. Documenting the situation helps protect your position and can provide evidence if things escalate.
- **Build a Support Network:** Find a trusted person—whether a family member, friend, or support group—to

help you navigate your concerns. It's often easier to speak up when you're not facing these challenges alone.
- **Ask for Help Early:** Reach out for support before things escalate. Sometimes, speaking to a healthcare provider or social worker early on can help you avoid major issues before they arise, reducing the risk of retaliation.
- **Set Boundaries:** Don't be afraid to say no when you need to. Taking care of yourself is essential to being able to care for your loved one. Express your needs calmly but firmly, and make sure your own well-being is part of the equation.

Recommendations for Professionals:

- **Create Safe Spaces for Caregiver Feedback**: Ensure caregivers feel comfortable expressing their concerns without fear of judgment or retaliation. Establish confidential channels where caregivers can voice issues or needs safely.
- **Foster Empathy and Understanding**: Professionals should approach caregivers with empathy, recognizing the intense emotional strain they're under. This understanding can open the door for better communication and reduce the fear of speaking up.
- **Encourage Advocacy**: Empower caregivers to advocate for their loved ones and themselves by providing tools, resources, and knowledge to navigate healthcare systems effectively.
- **Do Regular Check-ins with Caregivers**: Schedule periodic check-ins with caregivers to discuss any challenges or needs they may have. Regular conversations build trust and reduce the feeling of isolation.
- **Address Retaliation Immediately**: Take swift action if you become aware of retaliation or mistreatment towards caregivers, whether from other professionals or the

caregiving system. This sets a strong example that retaliation will not be tolerated.

Recommendations for Organizations:

- **Implement Anti-Retaliation Policies**: Clearly communicate and enforce policies that protect caregivers from retaliation, whether from staff, fellow family members, or outside entities.
- **Provide Caregiver Training**: Offer training programs for caregivers on how to advocate for themselves, their loved ones, and their needs within institutional settings. Knowledge about their rights and tools for self-advocacy will give caregivers more confidence.
- **Encourage Open Communication**: Create a culture where caregivers feel heard and valued, and where open, honest dialogue is encouraged. Caregivers should not fear asking questions or raising concerns.
- **Support Caregiver Resilience**: Help caregivers build resilience by offering emotional support, respite, and resources to manage stress. Recognizing their role as a crucial part of the caregiving system will reduce feelings of isolation and resentment.
- **Provide Resources for Legal Protection**: Connect caregivers with resources such as legal advocates or advisory services, so they feel secure knowing their rights are protected if issues of retaliation arise.
- **Clearly Post Complaint Processes and Escalation Procedures**: Caregivers need to be aware of how they can bring forward concerns in alignment with the structures of the organization and any reporting bodies. Resolution processes should include measures that promote healthy working relationships between staff and caregivers.

Recommendations for Policy Makers:

- **Create Legal Protections for Caregivers**: Advocate for stronger legal protections for caregivers against retaliation, ensuring that caregivers cannot be penalized for speaking up about concerns or for asking for support.
- **Fund Caregiver Support Programs**: Support and fund programs that help caregivers access resources, education, and respite. These programs should focus on helping caregivers avoid burnout and feel empowered to speak out without fear of repercussions. Third party mediators and dispute resolution teams such as Ombudsman's Offices need adequate staffing and funding to resolve challenges in a timely manner.
- **Develop National Standards for Caregiver Protection**: Establish clear, national standards regarding caregiver rights and protections, including anti-retaliation clauses, so that caregivers know their rights wherever they live.
- **Encourage a Culture of Compassionate Care**: Promote policies that encourage healthcare providers and institutions to treat caregivers with respect, fostering a supportive environment where caregivers feel safe and valued.
- **Facilitate Transparency in Health and Social Services Systems**: Create systems that allow caregivers to raise concerns and ensure that complaints are handled transparently and without fear of punitive action.

Key Takeaways:

1. **Fear of Retaliation and Its Consequences for Caregivers and Patients is Significant**: Fear of retaliation is a pervasive issue for caregivers, preventing them from seeking help, voicing concerns, and advocating for both themselves and their loved ones. Retaliation can take many forms, from losing

access to services, being labeled as difficult, or facing personal and professional consequences.
2. **Caregivers Need Protection From Retaliation**: Caregivers need legal protections, strong support systems, and a culture that encourages open communication without fear of backlash. Policymakers must ensure that national protections for caregivers exist, enabling them to speak up without risking their roles or their relationships with providers.
3. **Trust and Empathy are Essential**: Professionals and organizations must foster environments of trust and empathy where caregivers can voice their concerns and advocate for better care.

Summary:

The fear of retaliation is a significant barrier for many family caregivers who struggle with the weight of caregiving responsibilities. This fear prevents them from speaking up about the challenges they face, whether it's dissatisfaction with care, the need for more help, or concerns about their loved one's well-being. Without protection or support, caregivers are forced into a difficult position: remain silent to avoid consequences, or risk everything in order to seek better care for their loved one and themselves. By addressing these fears, through policies, education, and a shift in culture, we can help ensure that caregivers are supported, empowered, and protected, making caregiving a more sustainable and manageable role.

Chapter 15: Lack of Transparency

"My mom was at the hospital in emergency. I waited and waited to find out what the plan was but eventually needed to go home for a bit. It was getting so late and I was so tired. I just wanted to know if they were keeping her overnight so that I could try and get some sleep. I finally drifted off in exhaustion. I never did get a call. I made my way back to the hospital to get her or figure out what they were doing. Turns out they had her ready to be transferred to hospice, unbeknownst to me. Good thing I made it there in time."

When decisions are made behind closed doors without clear reasoning or communication, caregivers experience a lack of transparency. This can lead to frustration, distrust and feelings of being left out of important decisions, disconnectedness, uncertainty, and being unsupported and unimportant. Whether it's about the changes in services or policies, care planning, financial supports, medical decisions, and availability and accessibility to programs, the absence of transparency causes confusion and emotional strain for caregivers.

Examples:

Major changes, including potential layoffs and restructuring of programs and services, are made within an organization that provides essential services to support Philip and his caregiver sister Alice, with no explanation or communication to caregivers, leading to speculation and insecurity. The staff visiting their home are talking about the rumours and their fears that they could lose their jobs. This could mean that new staff or staff from a different agency altogether will be coming to provide care. Philip and Alice worry about what this will mean for them and the consistency of care.

A government program doesn't provide clear instructions or written information on how caregivers can access financial assistance or what is covered under their policies, making it difficult for them to plan financially. Further, Amy, who is the caregiver for her father, is given the wrong form and is unsuccessful at finding the correct one online. To add to the hassle, for Amy to submit the form she must also mail in the original Power of Attorney documents leaving her without it for other organizations.

Sarah has been caring for her mother with Alzheimer's for several years. When her mother's healthcare team changes medications, Sarah is never informed about the reasons behind the change. The doctor tells her that the new medication is just a "better fit," but without further explanation, Sarah feels unsure if it's the best decision for her mom.

Emily is a caregiver for her aunt who is being discharged home from the rehabilitation centre and transferred to community services. Decisions about her aunt's treatment, including changes to her rehab schedule, are made without consulting Emily. She only finds out when her aunt misses an appointment Emily was unaware she needed to drive her aunt to, leaving Emily frustrated and feeling excluded from important care decisions. Further, the missed appointment results in missed appointment fees causing further financial strain.

Recommendations for Caregivers:

- **Document Everything:** Keep a written record of important conversations, decisions, and changes regarding your caregiving duties. This can help you feel more in control and provide clarity if questions arise later.
- **Advocate for Yourself:** If you're not receiving the information you need, speak up. Ask questions. Request to be included in care planning meetings and communicate the importance of transparency in the caregiving process.
- **Educate Yourself:** Research caregiving options, financial assistance programs, and your loved one's medical conditions to stay informed and prepared for unexpected changes. Being proactive can reduce feelings of uncertainty.

Recommendations for Professionals:

- **Provide Clear Communication:** Always ensure caregivers are informed about decisions regarding medical treatment, discharge planning, or other significant care-related matters. Transparency helps caregivers feel supported and confident in their role.
- **Offer Written Plans:** Whenever possible, provide written summaries or care plans that clearly outline all steps taken in the caregiving process. This minimizes confusion and helps caregivers track progress.
- **Engage Caregivers in Decision-Making:** Actively involve caregivers in care discussions and decision-making. Make sure they understand the reasoning behind decisions and

how these choices may impact both them and the person they care for.
- **Be Transparent about Changes:** When changes are made to treatment plans, caregiving arrangements, or available services, communicate those changes promptly. Caregivers should never be left unaware of important shifts in the care dynamic.

Recommendations for Organizations:

- **Ensure Open Communication between Care Teams and Caregivers:** Create guidelines that ensure caregivers are consulted and informed when decisions are made about their loved one's care, including discharge planning and medical treatments.
- **Foster a Culture of Openness:** Establish policies that encourage transparency between healthcare providers, staff, and caregivers. Create opportunities for caregivers to ask questions and voice concerns in a supportive environment.
- **Implement Clear Communication Channels:** Make sure caregivers have access to clear, consistent information about care plans, financial matters, and any potential changes. This can be done through regular meetings, digital platforms, or written updates.
- **Provide Information Resources:** Offer caregivers access to information about support programs and services, and medical procedures so they can make informed decisions and avoid unexpected surprises.
- **Maintain Confidentiality and Respect:** Ensure that family members and staff respect confidentiality while also maintaining a level of transparency that helps caregivers feel included and supported.

Recommendations for Policy Makers:

- **Promote Transparent Healthcare Systems:** Advocate for policies that require healthcare systems to provide clear and accessible information about care plans, medical conditions, and available resources. Caregivers should not be left in the dark about critical decisions.
- **Establish Clear Financial Assistance Guidelines:** Make policies and financial aid resources more transparent and easy to understand. Provide clear instructions on eligibility, available services, and how caregivers can access support when they need it. Ensure that websites are user friendly with easy-to-find fillable forms and how-to guides. Hold information sessions that can help caregivers better understand programs and how to apply.
- **Encourage Family-Centred Care Models:** Develop policies that support a family-centred approach to caregiving, where caregivers are included in decision-making processes and provided with all necessary information to effectively manage care.

Key Takeaways:

1. **A Lack of Transparency Erodes Trust:** Lack of transparency can create feelings of frustration, isolation, and helplessness for caregivers, especially when decisions are made without their involvement. This can lead to an erosion of trust in the providers and organizations that are meant to support them.
2. **Communication is Key:** Clear, open communication about care plans, finances, and medical decisions can help alleviate confusion and improve the caregiving experience. Professionals, organizations, and policy makers must prioritize transparency in programs and services to ensure caregivers are supported, informed, and included in the care process.

Summary:

Transparency is critical in caregiving, especially when decisions regarding care, finances, and treatment affect the caregiver and their loved one. Caregivers need clear information to make informed choices and navigate the caregiving process with confidence. A culture of openness from professionals, organizations, and policy makers can foster trust and reduce the emotional burden on caregivers, ultimately improving the quality of care and the caregiver experience. Through better communication, clearer policies, and more inclusive decision-making, caregivers can feel more supported and empowered to provide the best care possible for their loved ones.

Chapter 16: Unprofessional Behaviour and Harassment

"There is no Employee Assistance Program for family caregivers. No handbook for how to navigate being labeled 'difficult' by professionals when you ask for help. No policies to protect you from retaliation when you question the care your loved one is receiving. As caregivers, we are expected to give endlessly, without the systems in place to offer us the same in return. But what happens when we ask for help and the very institutions we turn to respond with rejection, disrespect, or even punishment?"

Caregivers are vulnerable, especially when they face disrespectful, unprofessional, or even abusive behaviour from the person they care for, family members, or others in their support network, including professionals and systems. This bullying, whether overt or subtle, can take many forms: verbal abuse, condescending attitudes, exclusion from decision-making, blaming, or dismissiveness. Bullying can leave caregivers feeling undermined, silenced, demoralized and exhausted, shaking their fragile confidence and impacting their mental health. The consequences are far-reaching, leading to feelings of isolation and burnout. The fear of retaliation or simply not being believed often prevents caregivers from speaking out, leaving them to carry this burden in silence.

While caregiving itself is already a demanding role that requires patience, resilience, and emotional strength, the added weight of mistreatment can make it even harder to cope. Caregivers are expected to juggle complex emotional and physical responsibilities, but when their efforts are met with disrespect or disregard, it further undermines their ability to care for both themselves and their loved ones. These toxic dynamics often leave caregivers feeling devalued and unsupported, trapped in an environment of constant judgment and misunderstanding. Without adequate support or recognition, caregivers are left fighting battles on multiple fronts.

This chapter aims to shine a light on the often invisible issue of caregiver bullying, raise awareness about its damaging effects, and offer practical strategies for confronting and managing these challenges. It's crucial that caregivers receive not just empathy and compassion, but respect and understanding from the people they care for, their families, professionals, and the systems designed to support them.

Examples:

Fred is caring for his wife, who has dementia, at home. She is verbally and physically abusive at times, especially when he tries to gently correct her during tasks or assist her with bathing. This adds stress to an already challenging role and he worries that one of them might get hurt or that he may be accused of abusing his wife.

Amanda, who cares for her elderly father with dementia, calls a nurse to report a change in her father's health. The nurse dismisses her concerns, calling her "overly dramatic" and suggesting she "let the professionals handle it," making Amanda feel dismissed, unimportant, humiliated and unheard.

Tammy, legal guardian for her adult daughter with multiple physical and intellectual disabilities, is struggling under the weight of life-altering decisions regarding placement. She is doing her best to go through what information she has been provided with but has many questions still unanswered. Tammy is being heavily pressured by the service organization to make a decision within unrealistic timelines for receiving and providing everything that is necessary for her to make a knowledgeable and informed choice.

Candace, who cares for her son with autism, is constantly criticized by a social worker who says she's not doing enough to get supports and services because she doesn't do things like complete the application forms for programs quickly enough. Despite working tirelessly, Candace is told by the case manager that she should be "more resourceful," and "help herself", leaving her feeling exhausted and unfairly judged.

> *"I'm just trying to do the best I can for my loved one, but every time I make a mistake or ask for help, I'm made to feel like I'm failing them. It feels like everyone has a judgment, but no one offers support."*

Recommendations for Caregivers:

- **Know Your Rights**: Understand that you deserve to be treated with respect and dignity. Speak up if you are being mistreated and document any incidents of unprofessional behaviour.

- **Seek Support**: Caregivers should connect with support groups or counselling services that can provide emotional support and guidance. Being able to share experiences with others who understand can reduce feelings of isolation and offer practical coping strategies.
- **Seek Mediation**: Support for specific incidents, especially when there is a disproportionate power imbalance and dependency on the professional or organization, may require the support of a mediator or other outside neutral party such as an Ombudsman's Office. Seek out options for resolution that can preserve the relationships, especially if they must be continued.
- **Set Boundaries**: Establishing clear boundaries with the person being cared for, family members, and professionals is crucial. Caregivers should communicate their limits and advocate for themselves when they feel their needs are being overlooked or when they are being mistreated.
- **Practice Restorative Care:** Recognize that experiencing harassment or bullying can take a toll on your mental health. Practice self-care techniques like mindfulness, exercise, and ensuring you have regular breaks from caregiving. Even though caregivers may feel guilty about taking time for themselves, self-care is essential for maintaining both mental and physical health. Caregivers should carve out time for activities they enjoy and seek respite care when necessary to avoid burnout.
- **Recognize the Signs of Bullying:** It's important for caregivers to recognize when they are being bullied, whether the source is a loved one, family member, care or service provider, or external system. Acknowledging these behaviours is the first step in managing and addressing them.
- **Document Everything:** When facing bullying from professionals, organizations, or family members, caregivers

should keep records of interactions, communications, and decisions. This documentation can serve as a valuable resource when addressing concerns with management, healthcare teams, or policymakers.

"What if the professionals who are supposed to help your loved one, your doctors, therapists, social workers, are the ones bullying you, ignoring your needs, and making your life even harder?"

Recommendations for Professionals:

- **Listen Actively:** Show caregivers that you value their input by actively listening and addressing their concerns. Communication is key to ensuring a strong, supportive relationship.
- **Be Respectful:** Professionals should approach caregivers with empathy, respecting their expertise and knowledge about their loved one. Validate their concerns, and avoid dismissive or belittling comments. It's essential to provide clear guidance, support, and reassurance to caregivers, acknowledging their emotional and physical burden.
- **Avoid Assumptions:** Never assume a caregiver is uninformed or incapable based on their role. Treat them as equals in the caregiving process.
- **Provide Supportive Feedback:** Offer constructive feedback when necessary, but always in a respectful manner that encourages collaboration, not condescension.
- **Create a Collaborative Care Plan:** Work collaboratively with caregivers to develop a care plan that includes their input, acknowledging their role and expertise. This collaborative approach can reduce feelings of inadequacy

and increase trust between caregivers and healthcare providers.

Recommendations for Organizations:

- **Implement Anti-Harassment Policies:** Establish and enforce policies that prevent harassment or bullying among staff, family members, and caregivers. Make sure all caregivers know that their well-being matters.
- **Provide Training and Support Programs:** Train professionals to recognize the emotional and psychological challenges caregivers face and how to support them with respect. Management should create an environment where caregivers feel valued and supported rather than overburdened and undervalued.
- **Create Safe Reporting Channels:** Set up clear, confidential ways for caregivers to report any unprofessional behaviour or harassment without fear of retaliation.

Recommendations for Policy Makers:

- **Support Anti-Bullying Legislation:** Advocate for national policies that protect caregivers from abuse and harassment in healthcare, social services, and other settings, ensuring they are not punished for speaking out about concerns.
- **Standardize Training for Workers:** Encourage laws that mandate training for all professionals on how to work collaboratively with caregivers and avoid dismissive or abusive behaviour.
- **Provide Financial Support:** Governments should increase financial support for family caregivers through grants, subsidies, or stipends to help alleviate the economic burden caregiving often imposes. This financial support should

include the option for respite care and other necessary services. This promotes respect for the caregiver role.
- **Ensure Legal Protections:** Family caregivers should be afforded legal protections against mistreatment, discrimination, or undue burden. Legislation should ensure caregivers are not penalized for seeking assistance or for advocating for their needs.

Key Takeaways:

1. **Respect and Communication Matter:** Caregivers deserve to be treated with dignity and respect. Professionalism in healthcare settings is essential to maintaining a positive working relationship.
2. **No Tolerance for Mistreatment:** Caregivers should not tolerate verbal abuse, belittling, or harassment from healthcare professionals or family members. Setting clear boundaries is essential for self-preservation. Policymakers must enhance legal protections for caregivers.
3. **Need for Systems of Support:** Policies, training, and mechanisms for reporting mistreatment or bullying are necessary to protect caregivers from harassment and to ensure their voices are heard. Professionals and organizations must provide empathetic support and work collaboratively with caregivers.
4. **Self-Advocacy is Critical:** Caregivers must advocate for themselves, seeking out support when needed and speaking up when they are being mistreated, even when doing so feels uncomfortable. Caregivers need to recognize bullying behaviours, set boundaries, and seek support from other caregivers, professionals, and counselling services.

Summary:

Unprofessional behaviour and harassment within the caregiving environment can take many forms, from verbal abuse to exclusion to condescension to forced decision-making. Whether caregivers face disrespect from healthcare professionals, family members, or the individuals they care for, this toxic behaviour erodes their confidence, mental health, and ability to effectively care for their loved ones. Caregivers often feel silenced, demoralized, and emotionally drained, and may even fear retaliation if they speak out. It's crucial for professionals, organizations, and policy makers to create environments where caregivers feel respected, heard, and supported.

Conclusion

In toxic workplaces, employees often feel undervalued, unsupported, and drained, leading to stress, burnout, and poor overall well-being. These harmful environments don't just affect individuals; they ripple out to damage the organization itself, causing low morale, high turnover, and sometimes even legal consequences. Similarly, caregiving environments, where caregivers devote their time and energy to loved ones, are often toxic. Caregivers face emotional manipulation, unclear expectations, and an overwhelming sense of pressure to do more despite being at their limits. The personal, emotional stakes of caregiving heighten the toll, leading to burnout, isolation, and even physical exhaustion. These dynamics mirror what is seen in toxic work environments, but the difference is that caregivers can't clock out, they are tied to their roles in a way employees are not.

Yet, just like in a toxic workplace, change is possible. Recognizing these harmful patterns is the first step toward breaking them. Caregivers, as well as the professionals and systems meant to support them, need to address these issues head-on, whether through open communication, setting healthy boundaries, or reaching out for external support. If we hope to improve the caregiving experience, we must acknowledge the deep, structural problems that fuel the toxicity that caregivers face and make genuine, lasting changes.

This book highlights the interconnectedness of caregiver challenges and toxic workplace dynamics, revealing the complexity of caregiving and the emotional, physical, and logistical hurdles caregivers face every day. The struggles of caregivers are amplified by a lack of support, poor communication, and unrealistic expectations. These issues are not just isolated to caregivers, they are systemic. For the well-being of caregivers, we must rethink how we provide care, from individual strategies to systemic reforms.

Now is the time to act. To truly support caregivers, we must address the root causes of these toxic dynamics. For caregivers themselves, this means recognizing when they need support and when to set boundaries to preserve their health and well-being. For professionals, it means offering not just technical expertise, but empathy and tangible support that extends beyond just fulfilling tasks. For organizations, it means creating sustainable systems that foster collaboration and respect, where caregivers are seen and heard. And for policymakers, it's time to advocate for reform, fostering a caregiving culture that doesn't just ask for resilience but actively nurtures it through policy, support, and accessible resources.

Real change can't wait. Every system that exists to support caregivers needs to be restructured with empathy and respect at its core. It's not just about caregivers enduring toxic conditions or "getting through," it's about a full, collective effort to create environments where caregivers thrive, where their work is visible, valued, and supported. When we address these toxic elements and commit to reform, we make caregiving a more sustainable, fulfilling role for those who take it on. Together, we can build a caregiving system that is stronger, more resilient, and equitable for all.

The time for change is now. Let's rise to the challenge. Caregivers can't do it alone. Professionals, organizations, and policymakers must step in, act, and help build the systems that caregivers deserve, systems that offer recognition, protection, and sustainability. We have a responsibility to take this crucial step. Our future caregiving systems will depend on the decisions we make today.

Note from the Author

If you made it to the end, thank you. My hope is that this book and the conversations it may ignite will motivate positive change for caregivers. Caregiving is not easy and isn't always a choice. It is something that we do for many reasons and hopefully with love. Sadly, the challenges of caregiving can often become overwhelming and just too much. Caregivers need to be able to reach out for help and just as importantly have someone take their hand when they do. Friends, families, professionals and other supporters play a critical role in teaching us, guiding us, shoring us up when we need it and walking beside us so we are not alone. Even with this love and support, burnout can still happen. It happened to me. So to my fellow caregivers: you are not alone. I and the caregivers who shared their stories are with you. It is through these brave people willing to relive their experiences that we can raise our voices together. To those who read this book while it was in its various draft forms and provided input, suggestions for improvement, and encouragement, thank you for helping me make this what it is. I am forever grateful. To my professional colleagues: keep shining your lights and thank you for being there for me, especially when you didn't know you were. To my friends: I love you. Your love, support, encouragement, tough love, perspective, shoulders to cry on and arms to hold me up, have made gratitude every day possible. To my family: I am eternally grateful for all of your love and support for me and my boy.

About the Author

Julia Huckle is mum and caregiver to one son who came into her life through adoption when he was five years old. She is a proud Registered Nurse, coach, leader, and educator.

www.ingramcontent.com/pod-product-compliance
Lightning Source LLC
Chambersburg PA
CBHW050329010526
44119CB00050B/724